IN A FOREST, DARK AND DEEP

BY **NEIL** L**A**BUTE

★

DRAMATISTS
PLAY SERVICE
INC.

SPECIAL NOTE

Anyone receiving permission to produce IN A FOREST, DARK AND DEEP is required to give credit to the Author as sole and exclusive Author of the Play on the title page of all programs distributed in connection with performances of the Play and in all instances in which the title of the Play appears for purposes of advertising, publicizing or otherwise exploiting the Play and/or a production thereof. The name of the Author must appear on a separate line, in which no other name appears, immediately beneath the title and in size of type equal to 50% of the size of the largest, most prominent letter used for the title of the Play. No person, firm or entity may receive credit larger or more prominent than that accorded the Author. The following acknowledgment must appear on the title page in all programs distributed in connection with performances of the Play:

World premiere on March 14, 2011 at the Vaudeville Theatre, London
produced by Anna Waterhouse, Nica Burns, Max Weitzenhoffer,
Jay Harris, Josephine Genetay, Charles Diamond

SPECIAL NOTE ON SONGS AND RECORDINGS

For performances of copyrighted songs, arrangements or recordings mentioned in these Plays, the permission of the copyright owner(s) must be obtained. Other songs, arrangements or recordings may be substituted provided permission from the copyright owner(s) of such songs, arrangements or recordings is obtained; or songs, arrangements or recordings in the public domain may be substituted.

IN A FOREST, DARK AND DEEP recieved its American premiere at Profiles Theatre in Chicago, Illinois, on April 23, 2012. It was directed by Joe Jahraus; the set design was by Thad Hallstein; the costume design was by Shawn Quinlan; the lighting design was by John Kohn III and Bekki Lambrecht; the sound design and original music were by Jeffrey Levin; and the stage managers were Jordan Muller and Elisabeth Jackson. The cast was as follows:

BETTY ....Natasha Lowe
BOBBY ....Darrell W. Cox

IN A FOREST, DARK AND DEEP recieved its world premiere at The Vaudeville Theatre, London, on March 14, 2011. It was directed by Neil LaBute; the set design was by Soutra Gilmour; the lighting design was by Mark Henderson; and the sound design was by Fergus O'Hare. The cast was as follows:

BETTY .... Olivia Williams
BOBBY .... Matthew Fox

CHARACTERS

BETTY

BOBBY

NOTE

A slash (/) in a line of dialogue suggests the point of overlap with the next character's line.

IN A FOREST, DARK AND DEEP

Silence. Darkness.

We're in a room. It's not the only room in the place, but it seems to be pretty central. Doors and hallways leading off from this rustic space. An obvious front door. A loft up above.

Music was blasting before we started but now it's on the radio. Static but still loud. An '80s station.

Rain beats down on the windows and skylights. Tree limbs tap at the glass. Lightning flashes and thunder rattles.

After a moment, a woman appears above us. She's up in the loft space, moving quickly about as she fills an old box with mostly books. This is Betty.

She makes her way down a set of stairs and places the box by the door. Wipes her hands off on her shirt, turns the radio down and then spins to go back up the way she came.

The lights flicker and go out for a moment, then back on. Betty looks up, then goes and fires up a few candles.

Before she's done, a knock at the door. (By the way, this room and the others are full of stuff and the characters on stage will pack a lot of it up into boxes, bags, etc.)

The woman crosses over to the door, peeks out, then tries to open the door but fights the lock. Finally issues in a man — not soaking wet but he's damp. He carries a six-pack of Bud under an arm. This guy is Bobby.

BETTY. … I need … I gotta fix that door. / I owe you one for coming here tonight. *(A quick hug.)* God! Sorry it's so wet out.
BOBBY. Yeah. / No worries.
BETTY. No, seriously, I do, though. Owe you.
BOBBY. Fine. Gimme a towel, then …
BETTY. Honestly … *(She throws him one.)* I do.
BOBBY. OK, so you owe me. I'll jot it down on a piece a paper, stick it in the glove-box. See what happens.
BETTY. You do that.
BOBBY. I'm gonna. *(Beat.)* Call you up, some night at half-past nine when it's pissing down and see what's what.
BETTY. I would come.
BOBBY. Maybe.
BETTY. I would! God, that's not true … *(Hands him some cash.)* Anyway, here ya go.
BOBBY. No, that's … I don't need any …
BETTY. … Yes … just take it …
BOBBY. I thought we said that I'd …
BETTY. Bobby, no, it's not a big — it's only a hundred bucks. Take it.
BOBBY. Fine. Whatever. *(Smiles.)* Anyways, you're just paying me now so you don't owe me anything later. I know you.
BETTY. No, don't say … no. That's not nice. *(He pockets the cash. Snaps open a beer and takes a drink. Looks at his sister but can't hold her gaze.)*
BOBBY. Doesn't have to be nice as long as it's true. "The truth hurts," haven't you ever heard that one before?
BETTY. No.
BOBBY. What? You're lying …
BETTY. Not at all — is that a saying, or…?
BOBBY. Jesus, that's the oldest one in the book!
BETTY. Huh, well, I've never heard it.
BOBBY. "Truth hurts, don't it?" You've really never heard that? *(Beat.)* Come on, Dad used to say it. All the time …

BETTY. ... No ...

BOBBY. Oh, for Chrissakes! Come on! He did so.

BETTY. Then I don't remember it ... "Truth hurts." Hmmmm. No. *(Beat.)* I thought it "set you free" or something ...

BOBBY. That's insane. I mean, we sat at the same dinner table for, what, twenty years or so, off and on, and you don't remember the old man saying that? *(Imitating him.)* "The truth hurts, Bobby. Stings like a bitch. That's why they call it that ... the truth." He must've said it, like, a thousand times! At least that, if not more ...

BETTY. That's a pretty good imitation ...

BOBBY. Fuck that, it's spot-on. Spot. He was always saying that kinda shit to me.

BETTY. Well, then, you must've been a bad boy when you were younger ...

BOBBY. Yeah, right. *(Smiles.)* I did my share ... not a professional like you, but still. *(This makes them both smile. She reaches over and gives a little tussle to his wet hair. She checks her watch.)* You seriously don't know that phrase? "The truth hurts?" I mean, I'm just ...

BETTY. Bobby! Shit! Of course I know it, yes ... of course I do! I mean, please. Everybody knows that one — I was kidding! God! I was pulling your leg.

BOBBY. Really? You were?

BETTY. Yes, obviously. "The truth hurts," that is so old, it's a ... trust me. Yes, I remember him saying that. And not just to you. Others, too. Over the years.

BOBBY. So you did remember? You were just giving me shit about it but you do know?

BETTY. Yeah. 'Fraid so.

BOBBY. Oh.

BETTY. Sorry. *(Smiles.)* Truth hurts, don't it?

BOBBY. ... Ha. Bitch.

BETTY. Nope. Sister. *(He begrudgingly smiles then looks around the place. Takes it all in as he drops the towel on a countertop. Shaking his head. She wanders over to a wine glass, takes a sip.)*

BOBBY. Anyways ... *(Pointing.)* So this is nice. It's very what? Rustic, I guess. Cute. With all the little ... *(Points.)* Whatnots.

BETTY. Yeah. *(Smiles.)* It's good to see you ...

BOBBY. You too. Uh-huh. *(Beat.)* Hey, how'd you fuck up the car there? Your front side panel and all that?

BETTY. Oh, God, that's ... so dumb! I was, this is ridiculous, but

I hit one of those carts at the market. Shopping carts?

BOBBY. Yeah, I know what they are. You did, huh?

BETTY. Uh-huh. Didn't even see it — you know when people leave them out in the lot after unloading, they won't walk it over to the thingie where you're supposed to …

BOBBY. The cart corral.

BETTY. What?

BOBBY. "Cart corral." That's what they ask you to do — return them to the corral. That's the name for it.

BETTY. Really? I didn't … huh.

BOBBY. Used to work at Safeway, remember? When I was a kid. *(Beat.)* You used to come in and shoplift …

BETTY. True. *(Beat.)* Anyway, that's what I did.

BOBBY. Huh. Bet ol' Bruce was pissed …

BETTY. Not really. *(Beat.)* Pretty quiet about it, like usual. Like he is about most things.

BOBBY. Yeah? I guess so … he's kind of a pussy about that sorta stuff. Like … "life."

BETTY. Bobby, don't.

BOBBY. I'm just saying … *(Smiles.)* That's all.

BETTY. What?

BOBBY. He puts up with a lot of your shit.

BETTY. What does that mean?

BOBBY. Nothing. Just that. Dinging car doors and all your, ya know, conventions and stuff. Shit I'd never let you get away with …

BETTY. Yeah? You wouldn't?

BOBBY. Fuck no.

BETTY. Well then, I'm glad I didn't marry you!

BOBBY. Ha! *(Laughs.)* I bet you are! You and about a million other girls …

BETTY. And I don't go to "conventions." I'm not a salesman … they're conferences. They're a big deal, some of 'em, with people from all over the country speaking. Authors. / They're an important part of my job …

BOBBY. Yeah, whatever. / Anyways, I'm sure you got a deductible on it. The car.

BETTY. We do. It's not bad, really. A scratch … Bruce barely did anything when he saw it. I think he said they can "buff it out." *(Bobby nods at this, seemingly satisfied. He glances about the room, taking it all in. Betty watches him.)*

8

BOBBY. Huh. *(Beat.)* We gotta do all this tonight?

BETTY. I'd like to, yes. We've got people lined up to come see it and so we'd like to get it all ... anyway. *(Beat.)* We call it "semi-furnished" but this is a bit much ...

BOBBY. No shit! *(Beat.)* You shoulda told Hansel and Gretel to clean up after themselves. *(He picks up a book, studies the cover as he finishes his beer. Makes a face and drops the book back down.)*

BETTY. I know! It's a lot, right?

BOBBY. I mean, fuck. Yeah. Kinda.

BETTY. Sorry, but I just ... anyway, not all of it has to go ... most of the furniture can ... I'll show you. Sections. In fact a lot of it can stay, but ...

BOBBY. OK. Just thinking I coulda brought the Ford. Lots more cargo space.

BETTY. True.

BOBBY. You shoulda said something, or ... it's a long way to go back now. In the dark. *(Bobby lifts up a couple of magazines. Snooping. Drops them.)*

BETTY. I KNOW. This just came up. I didn't have anyone to — Bruce had a call he needed to make so he stayed with the boys ... and so I'm — yeah, I'm sorry. It wasn't planned so I didn't think about ...

BOBBY. Doesn't matter now. I'm here.

BETTY. Right.

BOBBY. You asked and I came running so let's ... just ... you know? Do it.

BETTY. True. OK. *(Looking around.)* Let's start in here and move outwards. Do upstairs last.

BOBBY. 'kay.

BETTY. Sound good? *(He nods his head and looks around. What to do first.)*

BOBBY. Fine. Work's work.

BETTY. Another thing the old man used to say ... one of his many "wisdoms."

BOBBY. Yep. *(Beat.)* Thought you might enjoy that — if you could remember it. *(Smiles.)* Idiot.

BETTY. That's me ...

BOBBY. Always doing some stupid thing. Right?

BETTY. ... Hey ...

BOBBY. It's true. When we were kids? That's completely true ... you were a total dumbshit.

BETTY. Yeah, well, maybe, but who's making more money now? You or me?

BOBBY. Fuck that, money's got nothing to do with being stupid.

BETTY. Oh, really?

BOBBY. Course not! That's the real "American dream." Don't matter if you're a dumb fuck, did shitty on your SATs, you can still drive around in a Cadillac and be a big shot …

BETTY. That's quite a theory there …

BOBBY. Absolutely true. I've made choices, led to where I'm at, what I get paid — same as you and where you are. This big college professor at some liberal arts program. So what? Point being, neither one of us ever left home. That's kinda pathetic …

BETTY. Hey, it's something — don't say that. I'm proud of what I've … doesn't matter. You think what you want. I'm happy with where I'm … plus, I'm the dean now, which is … *(He holds his hands up in mock respect. Makes a face.)*

BOBBY. Awesome. It's what you do. You make more than me because you're free in the summer and that's all. Same salary, less months. I figured it out on a calculator once.

BETTY. Ahhh. Thought it didn't matter.

BOBBY. It doesn't. I was just curious …

BETTY. Sure.

BOBBY. I was! I don't give a shit how much you make, Sis, I promise, or where you live or the house sits up on a hill. That's not me, what I'm interested in. *(Beat.)* We're both better off than any dude you meet on the street in Africa, and I mean any country they got down there. Any. That true or not? Seriously.

BETTY. God, the way your mind works, it's …

BOBBY. It's not racist.

BETTY. Oh, really?

BOBBY. It's not! I didn't say who: I mean any dude you see, white guy or a black one. Doesn't matter. Poor bastard was born in that shithole, he is just plain fucked and that's all there is. He's gonna get AIDS or, or, like, his hands cut off or sold into slavery — I'm saying in the past but they still do shit like that, taking kids for their armies? — it is a fucking nightmare down there. The dark continent indeed, right? Fucker's as pitch-black as the bottom of their own goddamn feet. You know? It'd suck to be African.

BETTY. Bobby. *(Beat.)* They're white.

BOBBY. What?

10

BETTY. The bottom of ... forget it.

BOBBY. No, what? What?

BETTY. Most African — all black people, I mean, in general — their feet are white. Or pink or whatever ... on the bottoms.

BOBBY. ... No ...

BETTY. Think about it.

BOBBY. That's ... *(Dawns on him.)* Oh yeah. That's true.

BETTY. See?

BOBBY. But ...

BETTY. I'm just saying. So ...

BOBBY. Whatever! You know what I fucking meant. It's an analogy.

BETTY. Yeah, but not one that works ...

BOBBY. I don't give a shit! Dark as their faces, then! Or the inside of their armpits. All the rest of 'em's black, correct?

BETTY. Yes. I suppose so.

BOBBY. Then there. Whatever dark spot you wanna pick. That's what Africa is like. BLACK AS FUCK.

BETTY. Fine. Jesus. *(Beat.)* Can we just...?

BOBBY. Anyway, that has nothing to do with the first part of what I was saying, anyway. *(Beat.)* First bit I said was about being stupid and a pain in everybody's ass ... which was very much your story. Right?

BETTY. What are you talking about?

BOBBY. 'Bout you as a troublemaker. That's what started the whole conversation ...

BETTY. ... I know, I know, but that's not ...

BOBBY. Lemme just finish. I'm just saying that a lot of things happened in our family — all this crying and tension and shit of that nature — due to choices you made. Guys you picked to run around with. You wanna say it's fine, no big deal, you were a kid, but lots of lousy times came from what you did. Mom moving out of the house for a while even, siding with you — I hated her for all that. Now, it's all crap that you've straightened out, I agree, still at the time it was pretty monumental to them as parents and us as a family ... but you just had to keep on doing it. You wouldn't listen to anybody in those days, not even Mom, after a while ... nobody could tell you shit. So. *(Beat.)* That's me just clarifying what I meant by "stupid" when I said it earlier. No offense. No harm done, I guess. Off ya go to grad school and life seemed to move on and then, poof! Outta nowhere, back ya come again, teaching

at our local college like no one remembers anything you did or all the, like, heartbreak you created ... *(Beat.)* Most normal people can't do that sorta thing: Wipe the slate clean and do it all over. I'm just pointing that out. *(Betty has stood by and listened to Bobby's little rant.)*
BETTY. Ha!
BOBBY. Seriously. I couldn't.
BETTY. I should've just called the moving guys! Didn't know I'd get a free Dr. Phil hour.
BOBBY. Hey, I'm just talking. You're the one who got into the pissing contest about status and paychecks, all that shit.
BETTY. I stated a fact, that's all. *(She turns and moves toward a stack of empty fruit boxes. Bobby watches her go as he cracks open another beer.)*
BOBBY. Right. *(She stops and turns to him. Tension is starting to build.)*
BETTY. I did.
BOBBY. You pushed a button.
BETTY. I thought it didn't matter.
BOBBY. It doesn't, but ... hey ... keep pushing.
BETTY. What? It either does or doesn't ...
BOBBY. You know what it does. *(Beat.)* Try it out on your husband there, when you get back home — who makes even less than me, by the way — see what that presses ...
BETTY. All I said was ...
BOBBY. You did the same thing you always do, any time we're together ...
BETTY. No, that's not at all what I ...
BOBBY. Yes, yes, you do, you get into the money thing a second after any argument starts or if we talk about the past, it's all ya got! It's your only ammo so you use it ... I understand what you're doing, I do, but it gets pretty old pretty fucking quick. You've made a name for yourself in your field, you read papers out loud to people every now and then, folks who don't give a fuck what you wrote, they just want to read their papers ... *(Shrugs.)* So what?
BETTY. Bullshit, Bobby! That is bullshit and I don't do that ... about my position. *(Beat.)* God, you are so like Dad that way, I mean really ... so goddamn judgmental! I think I'm doing fairly OK for me — as a woman, as, as a teacher, whatever! I mean, shit! *(She stares him down. Bobby shrugs and leaves it alone.)*
BOBBY. Betty, please. Fuck. Come on ... I didn't mean to start a

"thing." *(Beat.)* Can we just pack this place up, OK? I do not need to sit up tonight talking about us and where we are in life. I don't. You'd like nothing better than to show me your paystubs but I have places to be, things that mean more in my life to me now than a plaque on my door. I got work tomorrow and I know you're on your whatever-the-fuck-you-call-it so you can sleep in …

BETTY.   … Sabbatical …

BOBBY. Which sounds all important and religious but really just means you asked for time off to dick around and read novels, so …

BETTY. How did we come out of the same womb? I'm being serious, how?

BOBBY. We didn't. I was raised by wolves.

BETTY. True.

BOBBY. And you ran with 'em. Didn't ya?

BETTY. Who?

BOBBY. The wolves …

BETTY. Ha! You're funny.

BOBBY. Whatever. *(Beat.)* I mean, let's be true … you had a pretty good go of it when you were younger, like, just the number of guys you ended up with … for being, you know, a pretty average girl.

BETTY. … And what's that mean? Huh?

BOBBY. Nothing! No … we don't need to get into this stuff and I'm just your brother so what the hell do I know but you weren't like some gorgeous person when you were fifteen, sixteen. You were sorta chunky, even. Your legs were OK but you had a kinda dumpy ass. Not so big, but dumpy … *(Beat.)* Anyway, that's all.

BETTY. … Thank you …

BOBBY. I'm just pointing out some things …

BETTY. OK, I don't need any — can we get started? Let's just … I really need to get through this … shit … tonight. *(Beat.)* We can get together some other time and fight. *(He shrugs his shoulders and stops himself from going on.)*

BOBBY. Fine by me. *(Beat.)* When did this happen, by the way? Your little secret? *(She stops and looks at him strangely — it takes a moment before she speaks. He pops open another beer.)*

BETTY. … What do you mean?

BOBBY. I'm saying this cabin, when did you guys get into all this?

BETTY. Oh. Right. Just … a while ago …

BOBBY. Yeah? You never told me. *(Beat.)* Strange that you're buying up local … you know …

BETTY. What?

BOBBY. I dunno … property. That you guys are out doing that and, you know, in this economy yet I never knew it. Interesting.

BETTY. Oh.

BOBBY. I never heard a word. Per usual.

BETTY. Sorry. We've been busy, you know, with … and it's just one, OK? That's all. Just the one unit. *(Beat.)* We always wanted a place near the lake and it's great for us to use it … or rent it out as we … yeah.

BOBBY. But they've gotta be converted and shit, right? When you switch them over to being rentals and all that. True?

BETTY. They're … I mean … yes, but …

BOBBY. Huh.

BETTY. So? What?

BOBBY. I'm not saying anything.

BETTY. Yes, you are. What?

BOBBY. No, nothing, just that I'm a carpenter and, you know, do that sorta work, so it just seems … odd … that you'd buy a thing like this and don't even …

BETTY. That's not it at all.

BOBBY. No?

BETTY. No, it's not. Bobby. Bruce just wanted to do some of it himself and then we got to the point where it's — God, you're always so … fucking … ready to take offense!

BOBBY. Yeah, well … there's a lot of offenders out there. And I don't just mean women.

BETTY. Well, good. How progressive of you.

BOBBY. I'm not including the cunts I date. *(He smiles.)* That was a joke … *(He smiles and grabs a box. Starts filling it with books.)* Supposed to be, anyway. Probably not for someone as cultured as you …

BETTY. No. Probably not. Or someone, say, human.

BOBBY. That's not true, uh-uh. I knows lots of humans who woulda laughed at that. Lots. Only stuck-up pricks don't laugh at funny shit …

BETTY. Nice. Remind me never to accept an invite to one of your barbecues …

BOBBY. Ha! When would I ever have you over to my place?

BETTY. I was kidding.

BOBBY. Me too. I mean, about the "cunt" thing. But seriously, when? I stopped asking you to hang out with me years ago … Big Sis.

(They stop for a moment — they've been circling each other, looking for a place to strike. To move in for the kill. Betty checks her watch again; Bobby finishes his beer.) We should get going, if we're gonna strip this place down. *(Grinning.)* I will not be doing any windows, by the way …

BETTY. Yeah? You're old-fashioned like that?

BOBBY. Nah, I just hate looking at my fucking reflection. *(Beat.)* I feel like such a failure. Maybe if I made more money …

BETTY. Ha! *(She laughs.)* Stupid.

BOBBY. I know you are, but what am I? *(Beat.)* I told you, you're the stupid one, not me.

BETTY. OK, I got it, I'm stupid, cool — now can we get down to business?

BOBBY. Yep.

BETTY. Alright then.

BOBBY. It's your place, tell me what to do.

BETTY. Ummm, those books are fine, what you were going to do, that's great. I'm gonna grab these … along with a few other small bits and then I'll just need to wipe down the fridge and maybe the toilet and tub … oh, and there's a file cabinet that I wanted us to … *(Points.)* The loft. *(Bobby looks up the narrow stairs to the loft space.)*

BOBBY. Ohhh … *(Considering this.)* Why?

BETTY. What?

BOBBY. I'm just asking … why're you taking all the books and, and … the office-y crap?

BETTY. … Because …

BOBBY. It's none of my business, just tell me and I'll shut up. *(Beat.)* Doesn't matter.

BETTY. No, it's fine, I'll … I'm going to gift a few of them — the good ones, hardbacks — to the library and then, you know, I thought I'd take the rest over to, I don't know, the Salvation Army or somewhere. *(Beat.)* You know how I am about books …

BOBBY. Cool. I was just curious.

BETTY. And the files are — I mean the cabinet, not anything inside — is mine. From when I was going to make this my office … and then I just left them here but now I figure I'm — anyway! Blah-blah-blah. Right?

BOBBY. Hey, you said it. *(Smiles.)* So …

BETTY. Fine. So … yeah, let's just separate the textbooks and stuff out. You can do all of those. *(Points.)* I already started in the loft but these can go, too.

BOBBY. Got it. *(Beat.)* Where is this guy? What're we gonna do here, put the rest in storage or you wanna dump it all?

BETTY. Ummmm, he's ... how did you know that? That it's a guy who lived here...?

BOBBY. Oh, you know ... stuff. It's guy stuff. The way he keeps it and everything. Sorta in order but messy.

BETTY. Huh.

BOBBY. And dusty, too. Guys aren't, like, great at cleaning and shit. We arrange good, if we have to, but the actual lifting up of things and sweeping under and around? Not our strong suit. Plus, I don't think a girl is gonna pick out here as her first choice of safe spots ... way out in the forest. *(Beat.)* So, is it?

BETTY. What?

BOBBY. A dude who lived here?

BETTY. Ummmm ... yes, I think so. Bruce does most of the actual ... but yeah, I believe this was a man. Who stayed here. Yes. A boy.

BOBBY. Great. *(Looking around.)* Lot of stuff for a guy. Magazines and shit. Was he a fag?

BETTY. Bobby!

BOBBY. What? Gay, then. Fuck, you're so ... was he gay? I mean, look. *(Beat.)* The New Yorker.

BETTY. Why would you ask that? Or care, even?

BOBBY. I don't. Just curious.

BETTY. Yeah, but ... *(Looking around.)* Where does that come from? Whether he's...?

BOBBY. Just the little shit. Magazines stacked on the coffee table like that. That book there, tossed on the edge of the couch.

BETTY. So?

BOBBY. So — he wants me to notice what he's got. It's all a look, which is what gay guys do a lot. He wants me to be aware of it, but not too much. They call it "studied casual." I saw a thing about it once. On *Ellen* or one of those fucking shows. *(He looks at Betty.)* What? She oughta know ...

BETTY. Wow, that's quite a little ... theory ... you got there. About this guy.

BOBBY. I'm just guessing ... but I bet I'm right.

BETTY. I don't know. Sorry.

BOBBY. Doesn't matter. *(Bobby picks up a photo off a shelf and holds*

it up. Nice looking young man smiling in the picture.) This the guy?
BETTY. I dunno. I guess so.
BOBBY. Picture of himself in a silver frame. From Tiffany's. Guy's
definitely gay … *(Betty laughs and goes back to picking through stuff.
The picture is replaced by Bobby, who continues to browse.)*
BETTY. Stop! *(Waits.)* He's a second-year senior, that's all I know.
Working on his thesis and, umm … needed a quiet place to live.
BOBBY. Cool. *(Crack of thunder and lightning. Lights flicker again.)*
BETTY. Yeah, but he … I think Bruce said his family — mother,
maybe? — has cancer … not long to live or something like that.
BOBBY. Huh.
BETTY. … He took off and left his stuff here. Guess he figured
the deposit would cover the … you know … I'm not sure about
the rest, actually. *(Beat.)* We've got people now who wanna take a
look, so …
BOBBY. Oh. *(Beat.)* Fine, let's pack it up and we can toss it or
however you wanna do it.
BETTY. Great. So, you start with books and I'll do the … personal effects.
BOBBY. OK then. *(Beat.)* Can we turn it up? The music, I mean.
While we work?
BETTY. Ummmm, sure. That's … why not? *(Betty drifts toward
another part of the room — not really cleaning up so much as picking
through things. Bobby goes to the radio, searches for a station. Lands on
something. He moves back to the books and begins packing. One song
is just finishing — something from the '80s — and a song like U2's "I
Will Follow" comes on next.* After a moment, both brother and sister
are bopping their heads and moving a bit to the music. They notice and
then come together, dancing wildly [or as "wildly" as folks in their 40s
can dance] until the song is over. Bobby has to coax his sister to let loose
at times, but they both continue.)*
BOBBY. Come on! Go for it!
BETTY. What? I'm dancing! These're all the moves I've got! *(The
music ends. Next song is a slow one and they start to move to it as well
but come to a fumbling stop. They collapse where they are in the room.
Betty turns off the radio as they both suck down oxygen.)*
BOBBY. Hey! What're you doing? I was just starting to get into
it …
BETTY. Can't take it! Oh shit, I'm old! When did that happen?

---

* See Special Note on Songs and Recordings on copyright page.

BOBBY. You and me both … I gotta start to, you know, jog or some shit. I mean, one of these days … *(They both smile and then laugh. Still both out of breath.)*

BETTY. Well, good, we're getting lots done … *(Grins.)* Damnit! No more radio … come on.

BOBBY. Aye, aye, captain. *(Beat.)* Hey, U2 really used to fucking rock, didn't they? Like, back in the day. / When even that guitar guy had hair …

BETTY. Yep. / Bobby!

BOBBY. And before the other one started thinking he was Jesus or somebody.

BETTY. Ha! Who, Bono?

BOBBY. Whatever. Dude with the sunglasses. Guy decided to feed the world and, like, two albums later they sucked ass …

BETTY. Can you just … *(She waves him off.)* Go do those shelves.

BOBBY. Am I wrong? Bono. *(Beat.)* And "The Edge!" Not "Edge," no, "The Edge." I mean, who in the fuck calls themselves that?

BETTY. I don't know! I was busy with my own life the last … however long. I didn't follow U2 and all their … whatever. Exploits.

BOBBY. Well, good, then I can fill you in on all you missed. *(Smiling.)* Don't buy anything after *The Joshua Tree.* The rest is crap.

BETTY. Got it.

BOBBY. Just a little tip. I mean, seriously … *Zooropa.* The fuck is that? *(Pointing.)* And now, the books …

BETTY. Thank you! God, you're a piece of work …

BOBBY. Yeah, I know, I've been informed of this at various points in my life. In so many words …

BETTY. Ha! *(Smiles.)* I can only imagine.

BOBBY. You can more than imagine — you know both of my exes.

BETTY. This is true.

BOBBY. In fact, I think you sided with both, if memory fucking serves …

BETTY. The first one, absolutely. Second time all I said was, "Save yourself and get the hell out." Is that siding with her?

BOBBY. I think technically, yeah. *(They both laugh at this — time heals all wounds, I guess.)*

BETTY. You didn't speak to me for almost a year after Yvonne left you. Maybe longer. Up until that next Christmas.

BOBBY. I know.

BETTY. Which was hardly fair ...

BOBBY. You said some shit. Some pretty mean shit at the time which I didn't care for ...

BETTY. I know, but ...

BOBBY. Seriously, we can laugh about it now but during the breakup ...

BETTY. ... During the breakup you were being a really first-class asshole to her ... and she was getting sick of the 911 calls.

BOBBY. Maybe that was my relationship and you didn't need to have your nose in it ... *(Bobby swoops over and picks up a box. Begins to pile some books into it.)*

BETTY. Maybe your wife asked me to help ...

BOBBY. Maybe you were too fucking close to my wife for your own ... fuck it. Whatever. Let's drop it.

BETTY. Happy to.

BOBBY. I mean it.

BETTY. I do, too. Honestly.

BOBBY. We have hashed all of this out already a lot of times ...

BETTY. ... Too many ...

BOBBY. Maybe so, yeah. So let's just ... books. I am on it. Books.

BETTY. I'm gonna start in the kitchen now so we can keep this moving ...

BOBBY. Fine. Go for it. *(Betty moves into another area of the room — just a little kitchen extension — as Bobby continues with the books.)* ... who the fuck was this kid, Barnes or Noble?

BETTY. Ha! He was an English major ... I think.

BOBBY. Yeah, I figured that one out.

BETTY. Well ...

BOBBY. So he was one of yours, then? This guy?

BETTY. Yes. I mean, no, not really ... technically I suppose he lands in my ... but I'm not in that department any more. My office is now in the Humanities building. Across campus from there, actually.

BOBBY. Oh. But still ... English falls under your jurisdiction or whatever. Right?

BETTY. I guess so, yes. It's not really that ... "jurisdiction." I'm not a cop.

BOBBY. Whatever! Don't bust my ass over words or you can pack up your own goddamn boxes ... understood?

BETTY. Sorry. It's a habit.

BOBBY. Yeah, well … it's none of my business but Jesus! Give these guys a break, why don't ya? *(Pointing.)* This is ridiculous.

BETTY. What do you mean?

BOBBY. Kid spent all his lunch money on books! Let 'im watch a movie once in a while … no wonder he ran away!

BETTY. Why? What?

BOBBY. He probably made up that cancer story … about his mom. Truth is, he couldn't keep up with the reading assignments! Twenty-two years old and you ruined him for life with all your Tolstoys and Hemingways and those other douchebags.

BETTY. You really have, like, no respect for anyone, do you?

BOBBY. Sure, I do … not for writing fiction I don't, but people who have actually done things, yeah, I've got a ton of respect.

BETTY. What's that supposed to mean?

BOBBY. Guy who unclogged my septic tank a week ago Thursday? Him I respect. That cop who got shot out on I-94 last month by some Asian dude he pulled over? I respect him a lot. But some rich guy sits down and types up a little novel — *Great Gatsby* or not — who the fuck cares about him? I like people who work for a living … not some pack of actors or dancers or dickheads like that. Artists are a waste of fucking space …

BETTY. That is so … no … this is our usual fight we get into at, whenever … Thanksgiving or … so, no … not gonna do it tonight.

BOBBY. Fine.

BETTY. I'm not. NO.

BOBBY. Whenever you wanna start up again …

BETTY. Another time.

BOBBY. I'm gonna feel the same way. Exactly the same, I promise you.

BETTY. Fine, rain check then.

BOBBY. You got it.

BETTY. I mean … *The Great Gatsby*? *(Beat.)* I swear you go out of your way to say things that piss me off. *(Beat.)* How can you even…?

BOBBY. Only good part's when he gets shot.

BETTY. Who?

BOBBY. Gatsby! In the pool. I liked that.

BETTY. Oh, for God's sake …

BOBBY. Or when he lets that chick drive his car and she smashes into the other — *(Off her look.)* Yeah, I know. Do the books!

BETTY. Please … *(He nods and smiles, returning to the task at hand. Betty moves from shelf to shelf in the kitchen. Another blast of thunder. The lights flicker and go out.)* … Awww, shit. Come on!

BOBBY. You want me to do it?

BETTY. No, God … the box is just in the mud-room there … hold on. *(Hands him a flashlight.)* I got it. *(Betty disappears into another room. Flash of lightning. Bobby picks up another stack of books and he moves to an open box. Book on top slides off and falls to the ground. A picture slides out of the pages and onto the floor. Bobby picks it up, goes to shove it back into the volume. He glances at the photo. Stops. Looks at it again. The lights flicker and come back on. Betty enters again. Bobby puts the rest of the books in a box, then crosses over to his sister and hands her the picture. Walks away. She looks at it. Over at him. He has returned to removing books from the shelves.)* … What?

BOBBY. Nothing.

BETTY. No, what? Obviously you're thinking …

BOBBY. No, I'm not.

BETTY. Bobby, come on … BOBBY …

BOBBY. What?

BETTY. Talk to me. *(Beat.)* Please.

BOBBY. What would I be thinking? Hmm? What? *(He shrugs.)* You're the one with the master's. You tell me …

BETTY. Just say something! Ask me some questions or … just don't give me the silent treatment. OK? Don't be an idiot.

BOBBY. You're right — I shouldn't do that, I do not wanna be an idiot but you know what? It's hard not to be. It is difficult not to be the dumbshit of the fucking month when you're getting played. *(Beat.)* And I am, aren't I? Right now. Oh yeah …

BETTY. What's that supposed to mean? Huh?

BOBBY. You tell me. Sis. YOU TELL ME WHAT IS UP. *(Bobby continues to stack up books as Betty stares at him.)*

BETTY. I can explain …

BOBBY. Oh man, I hope it gets better than that.

BETTY. What?

BOBBY. That's the worst line ever. Ever. "I can explain." Of course you can! I bet you've had your explanation worked out since the first day you … well, whatever the fuck it is you're gonna tell me is going on.

BETTY. Nothing is "going on … "

BOBBY. Oh, really?

BETTY. No, it's not. I mean, not in the present tense. "Going" on, no, it's not.

BOBBY. Bullshit. You and your word games ... don't do the fucking Bill Clinton thing with me here, all right? Do not.

BETTY. I'm telling you the truth, Bobby. You did ask and so I am telling you.

BOBBY. Fine. Go ahead.

BETTY. I am. *(Beat.)* There is nothing going on in the sense that you're thinking. Honest.

BOBBY. Great. Don't worry about me. I handed you a picture, that's all I did.

BETTY. I know, but ...

BOBBY. The rest is your stuff. It's your shit ...

BETTY. That's what I'm saying, though, Bobby, I don't have any "shit" going on. It's just a photo. *(Holding it up.)* Look.

BOBBY. Of the guy. From here.

BETTY. Yes.

BOBBY. The guy from here and you.

BETTY. I know that.

BOBBY. Of you two standing there and ... you know.

BETTY. Uh-huh. Just "standing." *(Bobby motions for the rest, jumbling his hands together.)*

BOBBY. Close. Your faces are close together and he's ... his arms around your ...

BETTY. I KNOW. OK? Yes, I'm aware of that fact.

BOBBY. And yet you're ... all this time ... you're giving me the whole ... bullshit!

BETTY. What?

BOBBY. Oh, I dunno! He's a "second-year senior" and "Bruce is the one who actually ... " *(Beat.)* That's shit, all this is crap you've been saying to me so far! Right?

BETTY. ...

BOBBY. RIGHT? *(Beat.)* I mean, "cancer!" Come on!

BETTY. Some of it. Yeah. Yes, it is. *(Beat.)* This was taken at a ... we were at a seminar in, I don't even remember ... *(Turns it over.)* ... there's no date here ... must've been in, maybe, January or around there. At a conference. On semiotics.

BOBBY. Uh-huh.

BETTY. And nothing! He was in fact a second-year senior at the time and I … yes, I didn't tell the truth earlier. I knew him. Know him. Obviously.

BOBBY. Obviously.

BETTY. And … very bright and, and studying in my field so I was instrumental in moving him forward in the department, I mean, toward his degree. His thesis project. *(Beat.)* We are close here because of the cold — I was worried you'd overreact if I told you he was in my … so I didn't. I chose not to. *(Bobby and Betty face each other. Very quiet for a moment. Finally, he turns back to the books and starts packing.)* … What're you doing?

BOBBY. What you asked me here for … the fuck else am I gonna do?

BETTY. I know, but …

BOBBY. Didn't bring me out here to chat, I know that. Not to open your heart up to me … I get it, got it, so let's get done.

BETTY. Bobby.

BOBBY. I have a truck, I don't ask questions …

BETTY. … That's not why I …

BOBBY. Yes, it is! Please don't make me out to be a retard on top of the rest of it … do you mind? Just don't.

BETTY. I wanted your help. That's why I called you.

BOBBY. Yeah, to lift shit! Because you can't fit all this crap in your goddamn Prius, that is why — let's not make it into something more than it is, Sis.

BETTY. Yes, but … I'm … I asked you to, to …

BOBBY. To carry crates of this guy's fucking papers and underwear out to the truck, not because you actually need me. *(Beat.)* I'm a fucking pack horse to you, that's all … a drug mule. I-GET-IT.

BETTY. Not true. That is not …

BOBBY. Just don't! Please! Your condescending ways are always irritating but today … *(Indicating.)* Right about here. Just in the back of my goddamn throat right now.

BETTY. If you'd just let me … just …

BOBBY. I don't need any more explanation from you, I really don't. It's pretty obvious now … and the gory details are not what I wanna spend the rest of my night thinking about if you don't mind. OK?

BETTY. Alright. If that's what you … really …

BOBBY. Yeah, it is, thanks very much … *(Beat.)* Now I see why you're in such a fucking hurry. So you can get home to Bruce … and "the kids," you said to me! That's just … fucking … creepy and pathetic, just so you know. TO USE THEM LIKE THAT. I mean, goddamn! Your own children …

BETTY. I'm not gonna argue about this with you, Bobby … you don't know any of the …

BOBBY. And I don't wanna! At all. You and your shiny name on your desk can't make this look any better than it is, no matter if the fucking French do it all the time or not. Here in America we pretty much still consider this shit a commandment …

BETTY. What does that even mean? You're being …

BOBBY. It sucks, what you've done, that's what it means! SUCKS. *(Beat.)* If I was Bruce I would smash you right in the face …

BETTY. Is that right?

BOBBY. That is absolutely correct. Right in your goddamn uppity little nose …

BETTY. And we wonder why your marriages didn't last …

BOBBY. FUCK. YOU. *(Beat.)* Seriously, Sis, I mean that from the heart. Fuck you. You think I hit either of those bitches more than they did me? Huh? I was behind about two hundred to one. Yep. Easily. But it's all about the guy in that situation — one shot and you're fucked. One little tap and now you're a wife-beater. Scumbag. Meanwhile this girl you married — you used to adore every step she took — she is smacking on you like you're a foot-ball dummy … every day, just the way she was raised. Screaming at you and wailing away and ya know what? Too much of that shit and I don't care who you are. Anybody — and I mean anybody on this Earth — at some point, you're gonna take a swing at her in return. I promise you will. *(Betty listens to him and doesn't say anything back. Bobby stares her down.)* But I never cheated on either one of 'em. No, I did not. We maybe had problems and that's a matter of record …

BETTY. … Public record …

BOBBY. True enough, but I didn't fuck around. On anybody, in fact, that I ever dated, even when I was young and good-looking and had chicks bending over toward me, asking for it — if I was with somebody, that was it. I saw that shit through to the end … did not even think about another skirt until I was finished with the one in front of me. Seriously. *(Beat.)* Dad taught me that and it stuck with me. To this day …

BETTY. Well, great for you guys. So noble.

BOBBY. Hey, hey, I'm not talking about great or, like, being Superman here — this is just a common courtesy that we're supposed to do as people to each other. *(Beat.)* You're in a relationship, OK? You're with Bruce at this point, married with kids, that's it — you're not supposed to be banging anybody else. Get it? And not anybody else's kid, either. Thought students were a no-no ...

BETTY. We're not ... *(Beat.)* It was cold out. That is all. I don't know where you get the ...

BOBBY. Betty. Please.

BETTY. I'm serious! I don't need you doing any fantasizing for me, all right? I can do it for myself if I need to but I don't. I'm fine with my life and I'll tell you now: Yes, I lied about knowing him. Yes, I did do that. I was embarrassed. I'm sorry ... you caught me off-guard so I just ... he's a boy from the English Department who I have given some ... attention to ... and ...

BOBBY. ... "Attention" ...

BETTY. Yes, that's right! Believe me, you teach this stuff over and over, middle of what most people would comfortably think of as "nowhere" and someone shows up. My God ... he's actually read the material! He likes the subject, he can put two sentences to use in a paper ... it doesn't take much ... and you make a connection. A connection with another person. It's not carnal ... it doesn't mean you're in heat or about to run away from your loved ones — he's just some boy who understands what I mean when I talk about an author using metaphor and the animal imagery in *Phaedra. (Looks at Bobby.)* Doesn't matter. He's my friend. He's just a second-year senior who was trying to live as cheaply as he could and I let him use this place to stay for a while — both of us went to a workshop in Delaware and someone took a picture of us. That's not the end of the world. Or my marriage. Or anything else except your imagination on the loose and running wild ... *(Pointing.)* Look at the photo. Think about what I've just said and really study it. Seriously. *(She holds out the photo and Bobby looks at it but doesn't commit to holding it again.)*

BOBBY. Yeah, all right. Maybe.

BETTY. It's not "maybe," it's the truth.

BOBBY. Fine.

BETTY. Listen, I'm ... this is ...

BOBBY. Don't worry about it. You say that's it, then OK. We'll leave it there.

BETTY. Bobby, please ... I'm your sister ...

BOBBY. Fuck, don't use that as a measure of anything.

BETTY. Come on.

BOBBY. I'm serious!

BETTY. What?

BOBBY. That's … you throw that around when it's convenient for you, that little label … but otherwise it don't mean shit to you. *(Beat.)* Please.

BETTY. You are … God, you can be cold sometimes!

BOBBY. Hey, I learned from the pros.

BETTY. Are you … referring to me? Honestly?

BOBBY. You … and Mom … others, too. All of you guys growing up were icy bitches to Dad and me, don't act like you weren't.

BETTY. … Bobby …

BOBBY. And you were probably the worst of all. I mean it. *(Beat.)* Just old enough to hate a little brother, you had no time for me …

BETTY. That's not …

BOBBY. Always kicking me outta your room or, or, like, screaming in my face or telling Mom that I'd done shit — usually shit I hadn't touched, by the way — just to get me outta the way. Or if your boyfriends were over. You were a regular fucking terror …

BETTY. Oh, come on … that's stuff that everybody goes through! I mean, siblings do …

BOBBY. Maybe.

BETTY. "Maybe" nothing … why're you even…?

BOBBY. All I'm saying is you wanna act like you and me are all friendly now or when you needed your kitchen redone cheap, slip me a hundred bucks, that's fine, but let's not lie about it. *(Beat.)* We hardly know each other, Sis, and that's the goddamn truth. It is and it's pathetic. You and I are complete fucking strangers …

BETTY. Well, I'm sorry you feel that way.

BOBBY. I'm sorry you did so much shit to make me feel that way …

BETTY. And it's all my fault, right? I'm the one who's done everything wrong, is that it?

BOBBY. No, just enough to piss me off.

BETTY. You're impossible …

BOBBY. So they keep saying.

BETTY. I mean, sorry, but I see why you have so much trouble with dating and all that.

BOBBY. I have trouble when girls turn out to be whores or bitches. That's just me.

BETTY. Whatever, Bobby, let's not — why don't I do this myself? Alright? *(Beat.)* It's an obvious mistake, me asking you here.

BOBBY. Why? Because I've found out about you and all the — what'd you call it? — "attention" you've been giving out lately? Huh?

BETTY. ... No ...

BOBBY. I'm sorry that I find sin offensive.

BETTY. Fuck you! Stop saying stupid shit like that ...

BOBBY. Then tell me the truth — do that once!

BETTY. About what?

BOBBY. About this ... this whole ... *(Indicating.)* ... place you got here. Your love nest.

BETTY. You're crazy! Honestly, Bobby, you are just acting so ... completely ...

BOBBY. Bruce doesn't know a goddamn thing about what you're doing out here. *(Beat.)* Does he? I bet he's got no sense of what ... *(Betty stops cold and looks at her brother. He looks over at her and shrugs. Her face is slowly draining of color.)*

BETTY. ... That's ... you're so full of ...

BOBBY. True or not? *(Beat.)* Hey! I'm asking you a question ...

BETTY. What?

BOBBY. You heard me. *(Beat.)* Look at your face!

BETTY. There's nothing wrong with my face.

BOBBY. You don't look that way very often 'cause you hardly ever feel like you've done anything wrong, it's always the other guy. I know, I've watched you do this a thousand times before, but I can see it there in your eyes ... I'm telling the truth. What's going on here is as foreign to Bruce as all those fucking conferences you sneak off to each year ... *(Laughing.)* Fuck, he probably bought into this cabin thinking that you guys'd be ... some income and an investment, or ... like, for weekends and ... and ... *(Beat.)* No. That's not ... no. *(Bobby stops and looks around, taking in the cabin in a way he hasn't yet done. Looks over at his sister.)* ... Wait a minute. Wait a goddamn minute! Something's not right here. This is ...

BETTY. What?

BOBBY. If it was, you'd be doing this with him here and, and the kids'd be out running around — the whole line you fed me before about Bruce needing to be home blah-blah-blah ... that's made up. Isn't it? *(Beat.)* BETTY?

BETTY. No. It's, no ... he has a ... he's ...

BOBBY. You'd never have me over here, show it to me if you didn't have to … if you weren't completely fucking desperate! I know you!

BETTY. I needed your truck, I told you that …

BOBBY. Yeah, but … *(Stops.)* Fuck. "Rental," my ass. I bet that poor bastard doesn't even know about this place! Does he? DOES HE?

BETTY. … Of course. Yes. Bruce is … he's …

BOBBY. Yeah? Really?

BETTY. It's … it was a joint project. Yes, it's been rented out to … this guy … and it's now … but of course Bruce knows about it. I mean, of course!

BOBBY. I do not believe you.

BETTY. Jesus Christ! You're just acting … so … *(Bobby reaches into a pocket. Pulls out his cell phone.)*

BOBBY. Want me to prove it?

BETTY. What're you doing now?

BOBBY. Nothing, I'll just call 'im and ask if I should … *(Looks around.)* … I dunno, if he needs me to fix that door there or if I should just leave it. He probably wants it fixed. With all the new prospects coming by. Right?

BETTY. You're such a fucker, Bobby.

BOBBY. It's true. I would … lemme just ask. *(Betty doesn't say anything. He gives her a chance, then pushes a few buttons. It's ringing. Finally:)*

BETTY. Alright!

BOBBY. What? *(Pops the phone closed.)* Hmmm?

BETTY. Bobby, stop being a dick, OK? For just one second. Can you?

BOBBY. … If I really concentrate …

BETTY. Then do it. Please.

BOBBY. "Please" always helps. *(He smiles and puts his phone away. Turns back to Betty. She moves away and sits.)*

BETTY. You don't have any idea about my life …

BOBBY. No, I don't. We're not that close.

BETTY. Yeah, you said that already.

BOBBY. And I'm actually sorry about that.

BETTY. Sure you are.

BOBBY. I am! I always wanted you to treat me as more of a brother than you ever did — you can't look at me and tell me that's not true. Hmmm? Can you?

BETTY. … I'm … shit …

BOBBY. Doesn't matter. Now.

BETTY. Listen, I have made some choices that — you're right about this place. About Bruce. *(Beat.)* I'm doing this ... alone ... / investing for the ...

BOBBY. Betty. / Stop.

BETTY. I mean, he's ... no, I'm not even gonna try and lie about it to you. I'm tired of it.

BOBBY. Good.

BETTY. I helped him find it. The boy. A place like this, it was inexpensive and, and out of the way ... so we just ... we're ...

BOBBY. ... Which I'm sure you liked ...

BETTY. And yes, I paid a few months of rent on it. That's not a crime! *(Beat.)* It's not.

BOBBY. Matter of opinion, actually ...

BETTY. Is it? Really? Do tell, Bobby, I'd love to hear this one ...

BOBBY. You got one checkbook, right? A savings account or an IRA or some shit, correct? *(Beat.)* Betty! At home. Am I right or not?

BETTY. Yes.

BOBBY. You throw your paychecks together at the end of each month, don't ya?

BETTY. We do, but ... it's not like we're ...

BOBBY. Yep. Like most married couples do. *(Beat.)* And then you go decide to take some and spend it on yourself. You and your boy's rent and other shit, too, I'm sure, and that doesn't even register to you? Nobody else in your family's the wiser, so you think that means it's OK — you tell me if that's stealing or not. IS IT?

BETTY. That's a pretty broad ... come on, Bobby.

BOBBY. It's just plain math, Mrs. College Dean. And that's not all, either. I bet you're sure it's cool, the time you spend with this guy, running around to bookstores and, and ... fucking foreign films and all the shit you folks enjoy up there on the quad. You don't think those hours add up? Every meal you miss ... all the times that you spend away from your own kids to be with this guy, to laugh and wander and fuck this second-year senior — do not kid yourself, Betty! Your family's crying itself to sleep at night because they know something's wrong in that house of yours. You are a first-class thief, my dear, every day you spend with this dude. *(Beat.)* I'll bet Bruce even knows. Yeah. The back of his mind, he's gotta feel something ...

BETTY. ... I don't think so. No.

BOBBY. Then you're fooling yourself! Seriously, that's all you're doing …

BETTY. Bruce and I are … we're spending a lot of time apart these days. In the same house but you'd never know it. Different beds and, you know … all that.

BOBBY. … Oh. *(Beat.)* Well, OK, but still …

BETTY. That's just how life goes sometimes. I am not gonna blame him right now, when he's not here to defend himself but … we're … it's complicated.

BOBBY. It usually is.

BETTY. Yeah.

BOBBY. And perfectly simple, too.

BETTY. Ha! Yep. That's true, I guess.

BOBBY. Yeah. *(Beat.)* So you two are … what? Separated, or … I dunno. You tell me.

BETTY. Not yet. We've talked about a lot of … I'm not sure what's going to happen. I worry about the children and I need to … I'm not gonna just make some stupid quick choice that'll — but we're not gonna make it the way that things are now. *(Smiles.)* Not something I'm proud of, but hey …

BOBBY. No, I get it. It's usually hard to keep a marriage going when your wife's out there fucking somebody else.

BETTY. GOD! That is so mean! Jesus Christ.

BOBBY. Well …

BETTY. Can't you even try and understand where I am right now, how all this started? Huh?!

BOBBY. I am trying …

BETTY. That's bullshit! You're condemning me … that's all you ever do. You love to see me down and hurting and this is just … this is like nectar to you. I think you are loving this!

BOBBY. Hey, I didn't make it happen …

BETTY. Yeah, but you're sure glad it did.

BOBBY. I'm not surprised — let's put it that way.

BETTY. Everything is ugly through your eyes.

BOBBY. I'm just a realist, Sis. Don't blame me.

BETTY. It has never been just about … fucking … as you like to put it. With the situation here. I don't care if you believe me.

BOBBY. What is it, then? Companionship? Love?

BETTY. Would that be so impossible…? Hmm? That something like that might happen to me or come my way? Is it really? Am I crazy to think that I might find some … happiness?

BOBBY. Kinda. *(Beat.)* Seen you go through a lotta relationships … not just Bruce but guys for years and years and it never seemed like "love" was the number-one priority — I'm surprised it's even on the list!

BETTY. You're disgusting.

BOBBY. You're just trying to make it look all … cutesy and sweet now that it's obviously ended. Guy runs out on you and you're all dreamy about it rather than just calling it what it was. *(Beat.)* You had an affair, honey. You screwed a student. I bet it's probably against two or three rules up at the school there.

BETTY. Yes, it is.

BOBBY. It's sort of morally wrong, too. Not that I'm gonna throw that in your face right at this minute, but just so you know …

BETTY. That's a big word for you to be using.

BOBBY. Really? I don't think so — I have plenty of morals. Always have. You used to skip out on Vacation Bible School. Not me.

BETTY. So you're a religious guy now? That's …

BOBBY. I didn't say "religious." Who said that? *(Beat.)* I'm saying I have a moral core, a center that doesn't waver … and that's a fact about me, whether I swear too much or I've been divorced or, or whatever … lose my cool in a bar once in a while, it doesn't change the essential nature of me as a man. What I believe. How far I'll go or not and what I know is just absolutely against the laws of mankind. Not God, not that but what every person should be willing to stand up and say "no" to. I've got that in me and I'm not so completely sure that you do, Betty … not at all.

BETTY. Really? You know that about me?

BOBBY. I know some things. I do. *(Beat.)* I saw a program on television the other night — I got the History Channel on, like, 24/7 — it was one of those shows where it has a real person on it. A documentary. About a guy who comes home from the war, and I'm saying just recently, from Iraq … and he was shot in the spine, he's a cripple now and it follows his journey back. Recovery and his doing rehab, all that shit. Whole time I'm watching I'm looking at his wife next to him. Young, beautiful girl. She's a rock — helping him with his pee-sack and they can't have sex unless he has a shot or, like, one of those pumps in his dick but she's still there, tucking a pillow in behind his … and all I'm thinking, the entire show, is how much I'd like to fuck her. Seriously. Find out the place they live and go down there and get her outta that situation. I mean, she's gotta be sick of being on top by now, right?! Now that's a kinda sick thought, I know, but the point being … I won't do it. I'm not gonna track them down or pretend to run into her in a bar or, or at Chili's and be, like, "Oh, hey there … " Because it would be wrong. She loves this fucking guy who can't sit up straight and shits in a can. He is her man so who am I to go get in the middle of that? Nobody, that's who. It'd be a bad thing and a sin and so she's now off-limits. *(Beat.)* See?

BETTY. What the hell am I supposed to get outta that story? Huh?

BOBBY. I think it's pretty obvious …

BETTY. Not to me, Bobby. Honestly.

BOBBY. Yeah, because you've got no sense of fucking morality, Sis. That's the trouble.

BETTY. OK, this is getting a little too …

BOBBY. I'm serious!

BETTY. Just stop now, OK? Stop. I get it.

BOBBY. No, I don't think you do, no, and here is why: 'cause-you-keep-on-doing-it.

BETTY. What?

BOBBY. You keep going out there and having more and more adultery.

BETTY. Bobby, just … and that's not even a word. Not the way you use it …

BOBBY. Bullshit, is too! Yes! "Adultery."

BETTY. It's not! And I'm just … stop it! STOP!

BOBBY. We can stop — let's pick up your precious files and I'll be on my fucking way. Get away from your little house of filth …

BETTY. You're not here because of files, OK?! That's obvious, so just … stop. Please.

BOBBY. Then why? Huh? Why am I here?

BETTY. Because …

BOBBY. Yeah, go on …

BETTY. Because I needed somebody around while I did this, went through all of it — you're right, I obviously couldn't have Bruce do it, no. So, who else? All I got is you … like it or not, we're family. We're stuck with each other.

BOBBY. Ha! Too bad you don't have any friends …

BETTY. I know.

BOBBY. I was kidding.

BETTY. No, it's kind of true. I'm … women don't like me usually;

as friends, coworkers, that sort of thing. Some women are just like that. I do better around men — and I mean just as acquaintances.

BOBBY. Right.

BETTY. Women seem threatened by me.

BOBBY. Maybe because you fuck most of their men. That gets annoying after a while …

BETTY. That's not true!

BOBBY. Pretty much.

BETTY. I do not! When I was younger, yes, I was a bit … wild, or … I don't know. On the prowl. But that stopped years ago … I've been whatever but I did try. Got my head on straight after college and I tried for a while there, to make my marriage work and all that. *(Beat.)* I really did …

BOBBY. Except for this new guy. Your second-year senior.

BETTY. Yes, that's true. He's different …

BOBBY. I doubt it.

BETTY. And what's that mean?

BOBBY. Look me in the eye — tell me he's the only one since you've been with Bruce. *(Beat.)* Seriously. Try and tell me that …

BETTY. Bobby, no … I'm not gonna …

BOBBY. Say it. You tell me and I'll believe you.

BETTY. This is not the … I'm … *(Bobby walks over and stands in front of his sister. Waits for her to say something. Faces inches apart. He puts his finger against her chest, pushing her. Again. And again.)*

BOBBY. Say it. Go on, say it. SAY IT. SAY IT!

BETTY. STOP! *(Beat.)* Alright, yes. He's a … this was something else. Something wonderful.

BOBBY. Ha! Bullshit. Bull-fucking-shit — the lies you tell yourself to get by! Fuck, you're amazing!

BETTY. I'm not lying …

BOBBY. Fuck you're not …

BETTY. I'm not!

BOBBY. Yes, you are! Yes!

BETTY. IT'S NOT A LIE! IT ISN'T, BOBBY!! NO!!! *(Betty explodes and smacks Bobby on the cheek. Hard. This stops him cold. A moment of dead silence passes between them.)*

BOBBY. … Fine.

BETTY. Fuck. Sorry. *(Beat.)* Look, you don't know him, OK? He's … so funny and just, well, really sweet. Very smart and yet not all — he's just a very special person.

BOBBY. I'll bet.

BETTY. He is! Jesus, can't you ... I mean, try and respect me at least, if nothing else.

BOBBY. Why? *(Beat.)* I mean, why start now? *(Bobby waits for her to respond but she doesn't. Silence.)* I'm not gonna lie here — I don't at all respect you, what you've done with your life or, or career and certainly not the way you run around with your pants down. *(Beat.)* You've always been like that and people talk about it behind your back and it makes me sick. Like, physically sick. *(Beat.)* ... Why do I need to pretend I like that or respect you? I am not gonna. No.

BETTY. Then fine. Just go. I can finish this by myself ... I'm tired now, so ...

BOBBY. Fine. *(Tosses money back at her.)* Doesn't matter to me.

BETTY. Good. Thanks for nothing.

BOBBY. Hey, hey, thank your own fucking self, you bitch ... shit! Don't blame a single thing on me here. You got that? NOTHING. You're the one who's done this ... brought all of this down on your own head.

BETTY. Whatever ...

BOBBY. You're goddamn right, "whatever." *(Beat.)* I can't help it that not even a length of chain could keep those fucking thighs of yours closed. The first whiff of cock and they part like the goddamn Red Sea, so do not point a finger at me! OK?!

BETTY. You're sick.

BOBBY. I may be sick — I might also be the only guy in a three-town area that you haven't fucked, so that's something — 'cept Bruce.

BETTY. JUST GO!

BOBBY. I am, you bitch! Shut your goddamn mouth!

BETTY. Get out, you fucker! You fucking ... AAAH!! *(Bobby shakes his head, agreeing with this assessment.)*

BOBBY. Call me whatever you want — point is you know I'm not lying. You've brought a lot of guys to their knees with that smile of yours ... over the years ...

BETTY. ... Bobby ...

BOBBY. Don't say that you haven't. *(Beat.)* You're just adding to the collection with a new guy. Student, teacher, it's all the same to you. Right?

BETTY. Let's not ... I really don't have time for this now. All your ... foul ...

BOBBY. Yeah, why think about the past? You sure as hell don't learn from it, so ...

BETTY. Oh, stop! Please! Just ... just don't. This is the kind of shit Dad would do to me ... piss me off by bringing up all the things I'd done and rub my nose in it!

BOBBY. Hey ... I'm sorry you got involved with a married man once upon a time! I'm very sorry. Wasn't a fairy tale with a happy ending, though, was it? You two didn't ride off into the sunset or anything even close to that. *(Beat.)* Not that you cared.

BETTY. ... Please stop ... please ...

BOBBY. Don't cry now, Sis, 'cause you didn't do shit about it at the time and I know that to be a fact. Back when you could've done a thing or two, spared this guy his fucking dignity, at least, you did nothing ... turned your thumb down like a Roman senator and sent the poor son-of-a-bitch to his grave ... *(Beat.)* You fucked that guy — Mr. Freeman or whatever his name was — you were dicking around with him at seventeen and got him booted out of his job at the high school. That's not just hearsay ... those are cold, hard facts. You wouldn't listen to Dad and that's what it got you.

BETTY. I know.

BOBBY. You were a fucking skank and you let a man throw himself on his fucking sword for you and what'd you do about it? Huh? WHAT?

BETTY. You know what! Say it if you need to ... GO AHEAD. *(Beat.)* He was an adult, by the way. Alright? Just so you know ...

BOBBY. He threw his family away, "by the way!" His kids and every chance he had for a normal sort of life. Kids I used to play with, work that he planned his whole life for ... and you let him! Let him blab to his friends about it and think you guys would be going to Vegas and that whole deal. The guy wanted to marry you ... can you even imagine what must've been going through that head of his?! The fucking delusions he was living off of ... and all because of you. Because of the way some teenager was sucking his cock. *(Beat.)* We all knew you hated us — Dad and Mom and me — we figured that part out, but you didn't have to take it out on the whole goddamn world. You coulda let that guy go and he maybe woulda limped on back home to his family in the end, maybe even kept his job — but instead you ground him down, let him come off like some fucking jackass in front of everybody and ... God, it was just ugly and pathetic and, like, sad in the end. I

35

don't know if you've just … maybe blocked it out or not, but shit, Betty, I will never forget what that dude was like the last time I saw him. You know? He was a fucking ghost. That is what you did by living free and easy and not having time to let your parents tell you one goddamn thing about life. Nope, you knew everything and just couldn't be bothered in those days … so that's what you did. You destroyed a whole person … and I'm not sure he's ever bounced back from that. There's every chance he didn't … *(Beat.)* I dunno what happened to any of 'em, him or that mousey wife of his or, or any of those three kids. I never saw them again after that summer, but I did happen to be on the street when she drove 'em away … I was there on my bike as they passed me. She was looking straight ahead and that girl of theirs … I forget her name now …

BETTY. … Ellie. His daughter's name was Ellie.

BOBBY. Huh. Look at that — good for you.

BETTY. Go on … tell me …

BOBBY. Ellie was looking out the window and she was staring at me. Not accusing or, or, like angry or anything, but just a look of, like, despair or something. Of having had to grow up, straight up into being an adult, over the course of those few weeks or months or whatever. It was like it was her but also her as an adult, looking out at me. Yeah. *(Beat.)* It was spooky … *(Bobby and Betty stand still for a moment — a cell rings at that moment, breaking the tension. Lightning strikes. Betty goes to her purse, sighs, then answers.)*

BETTY. … Hey, honey. Yes. Uh-huh. No, I know … I know it's getting late. No, they don't need to stay up and see me, I'll get 'em up in the morning and ready for school … it's fine. I know. Yes. What? I'm almost done, I'm just … *(Looks at Bobby.)* No, I just want to finish up these few notes on the bibliography and then I'll, yes … be home after that. Right. Oh, well, no, I'm not at my desk, that's why … no, I'm over at the, can I please just … no, I've gone over to the student union building for a cup of coffee. Yeah. Sorry. Don't worry, it's whatever. You don't have to … this whole thing is, fine. I thought we were not gonna do this to each other. All the questions and, and … then OK. I'm getting a coffee and I'll be back there and I'll finish up. Then home. Alright? *(Beat.)* Do what? When? Bobby called you earlier … oh. I wonder what about? Hmmm. OK, yeah, no, I will. *(She turns to Bobby again.)* Well, if he hung up then it was probably a mistake. Yeah. OK. Yes, I'll tell "that fucking loser" not to call you for any reason when I see him. Alright. G'night. Yeah, I'll be careful … yeah, I can see that it's wet. Yes. Bye. *(She clicks off her phone and returns it to her purse.)*

BOBBY. Charming …

BETTY. Yep.

BOBBY. What a fucking asshole …

BETTY. I'm sure you did something to earn it. I mean, in his eyes …

BOBBY. Whatever. Guy feels that way about me and he's got no idea about the woman that he shares his wedding bed with … pretty fucking typical. Ha!

BETTY. Doesn't matter.

BOBBY. Yeah, to you maybe.

BETTY. Just let it go. You can never let things go …

BOBBY. Can too.

BETTY. … Hardly …

BOBBY. Fine. Fuck if I care.

BETTY. … And we're not sharing anything much anymore. Certainly not the wedding bed.

BOBBY. Yeah, you say that but how the fuck do I know what you're doing?

BETTY. You heard me talking to him, didn't you?

BOBBY. So what? You sound like a million other married couples …

BETTY. Really?

BOBBY. Pretty much. Together but, you know … just barely. Everybody sounds like they'd rather be with somebody else these days.

BETTY. I don't even know what to say to you …

BOBBY. I'm not saying you guys aren't … but you just stand there and lie to him. Just as easy as breathing. "Coffee" and "over at the student union" like it doesn't matter to you, like the truth is just something that happens once in a while, like one of those comets that flies by every hundred years! *(Illustrates.)* Whoosh! I mean, God, don't you even wanna try anymore? Fuck …

BETTY. You're here with me right now … you know what I'm dealing with. How do you figure I'm gonna start telling the truth right now? Hmm? How?

BOBBY. You gotta start sometime! You have to, I dunno, just fight your way out of the … thicket of lies you weave and … just …

BETTY. Yeah? OK, here. Truth is I've had a few flings over the years … men at work or people from … doesn't matter. Guys. I'm quite sure — no, in fact I know — Bruce has done the same thing, how long or how many I'm not certain but before me. So there.

BOBBY. Bruce? No … that pussy? I don't believe it.

BETTY. Yeah. 'Fraid so. *(Beat.)* Yes.

BOBBY. … Jesus … I'd've never … wow.

BETTY. First one I found out on my own, I was six months pregnant. I was trying, too, wanted to be his model bride and to put my earlier days behind me — not so easy living in the same town — but I was now a college graduate and a teacher and had even gotten married and had a kid. Just like they tell you to do, in stories and on the TV. And he was sleeping with his secretary. Just like they tell men to do, in stories and on the TV. *(Smiles.)* That was how it started up again … me paying him back, even while I was carrying his baby. I mean, it's the perfect way not to get pregnant, right? Going to bed with a guy when you're already — and believe me, there's a lot of men out there who are very into that idea. Very. So I started up doing that and I guess we just … I dunno. We just never … stopped. Bruce and I have gone our own ways but we pay the mortgage and keep the lawn mowed and most everybody in town figures we're doing just fine. *(She turns to Bobby.)* I don't care what things you say about this guy … he is different and special and a really … I could just go and be myself with him! Be real and funny and just a, like, a total woman and he was completely into me. Me as a person and a writer and it didn't matter if I was ten pounds too heavy or older or any of that sorta crap. He's kinda perfect. That is the truth of it. Younger than me and from this well-to-do family but just the sweetest, nicest guy you could ever wanna — *(Her eyes are welling up with tears.)* He was not "nothing" to me. You should know that. Believe what you wanna about me and, and however you feel about the situation, but this was not nothing.

BOBBY. … I see.

BETTY. I'm just saying. OK? He was special. In my mind …

BOBBY. I hear ya. I mean, if … you're …

BETTY. … Anyway …

BOBBY. No, that's … if that's the case, then you should do something about it. *(Beat.)* Fuck what I say or people think — that's how ya used to be with all of us — so go do that. Just, you know … go for it.

BETTY. I can't …

BOBBY. Sure, you can. *(Beat.)* I'm serious here. If he's that fucking great, then go …

BETTY. It's over, Bobby, let's just … I wanna do this and get home, so …

BOBBY. No, I think you should go after him, you feel this way about it.

BETTY. Bobby.

BOBBY. Betty, fuck, change your life!

BETTY. Why're you … I thought it was a sin?

BOBBY. Yeah, but, no, this is … but there are circumstances on occasion. Things that make it more OK than other times.

BETTY. … That's convenient …

BOBBY. I'm saying it's true — you've convinced me here that you love this guy, that you're wanting more than just a fling so I think you should, you know … go and, and …

BETTY. I can't now …

BOBBY. That's not true! People do this.

BETTY. I'd like to, but it's not …

BOBBY. Yes, you can, Betty! Yes! *(Beat.)* I'd be a lot more proud of you, I'll tell ya that. Doesn't matter if you break up the family because once they know, the kids can make a new life, one that's honest and they'll be able to be more free to love you. Even Bruce would be, he would … and you could do what you want without this secret life weighing you down! Every day, you having to pretend and all that, instead you'd be past that and be your own … it's true … go get a divorce and do it right!

BETTY. Bobby, I'm telling you I can't, OK?! Why don't you just stay outta my business for once and let me decide if I'm …

BOBBY. Because you do nothing right! You always do the easy thing, the shit where it's no big deal to keep up the facade and forget about anybody else's needs … why not just once think of someone else!! Huh?! Don't always fucking choose yourself …

BETTY. I'm not doing that!

BOBBY. Yeah, you are … you always are …

BETTY. No, Bobby, I'm not!

BOBBY. This would be as much for them as it'd be for you — your kids need you to — everybody wins if you'd just … go and …

BETTY. Bobby, stop! Stop it!!

BOBBY. Think about it, it's the only …

BETTY. STOP! STOP IT!! JUST FUCKING SHUT UP!! I NEED TO BE LEFT ALONE, GODDAMNIT! *(Bobby hears this and refrains from any further talking. He holds up his hands as if to surrender.)*

BOBBY. Hey, whatever you wanna do … far be it from me to ever make you think twice …

BETTY. No, I actually have thought this through, every last bit of it … and it's not possible for me to … this isn't some …

BOBBY. … Just forget it … I mean, listen to me! I'm telling you to dump your husband and your kids … what the fuck is that?! I was trying to be nice to you for once, to say, "Go for it" and run off with some dude I don't even know, if it makes you happy … and you can't even do that right! I think you wanna be unhappy's what I think!!

BETTY. You don't know anything …

BOBBY. I know it can't be that bad, whatever was the reason this guy left here in such a hurry … I know that you could reach out to 'im and probably turn things around if you wanted to …

BETTY. … No …

BOBBY. That's not true! You could! He's a kid and he's probably all mixed up, dealing with you as a woman and, like, a mentor at school, that's a lot to take in …

BETTY. I know, but … he's …

BOBBY. But you can do it! Call him, Betty, call 'im right now … come on!

BETTY. I SAID "NO!"

BOBBY. You won't! That's all, you won't, 'cause you're a stubborn fucking bitch, that's why …

BETTY. Bobby, you don't know what the fuck you are talking about … so just …

BOBBY. Yes, I do, you're just being cunty about this, like usual!

BETTY. I'm not! Fuck! Listen to me, I'm …

BOBBY. Call him up or shut the hell up about it, OK? That's all I got to say about this …

BETTY. I CAN'T CALL HIM UP, ALRIGHT! I CANNOT!! I WANT TO, I WOULD LOVE TO, BUT I CAN'T … *(Beat.)* He's not … he's dead. He died and so I can't …

BOBBY. … What? The fuck are you talking about?

BETTY. I just said it, don't make me say it anymore.

BOBBY. He's dead? This guy … your … what?

BETTY. Yes. *(Beat.)* He didn't leave me. We didn't have a fight and break up, I never for a minute said that to you … no. He died and so … so, I'm …

BOBBY. Yeah, but … I mean …

BETTY. He was ... three days ago. That's why I'm here now. Because that happened ...
BOBBY. Oh.
BETTY. So.
BOBBY. Shit.
BETTY. Pretty much. *(A rumble of thunder and lightning. The lights flicker on and off. Why not? It's perfect timing.)*
BOBBY. That's fucking ... I'm sorry. Betty.
BETTY. Thank you.
BOBBY. No, I seriously am ... that's ...
BETTY. It's unbelievable, that's what it is. It is right off the charts awful and, like, it's like a curse or something ...
BOBBY. ... No ... don't say ...
BETTY. Well, feels like it! Like God's punishing me for being happy for one minute ... for finally finding someone ... who I'm ... *(Betty has no more to say. She sits there looking blankly at her brother, who seems troubled by the news.)*
BOBBY. I mean ... Christ. He's...? *(Beat.)* Goddamn.
BETTY. That's why I needed you here. Not for the books or the ... the, you know ... stuff. In the back of my mind I thought I could go ahead and tell you but we always get — in the end I didn't feel safe enough to do that ... *(Beat.)* You know how we are. Two minutes together and we're ... tearing at each other's throats ...
BOBBY. Yeah. Usually.
BETTY. Almost always.
BOBBY. True. But, I mean ... this is different.
BETTY. Is it?
BOBBY. Of course!
BETTY. Maybe. Somehow I figured it'd just end up the same stuff for us ... another thing to misunderstand and fight about ... and ...
BOBBY. ...
BETTY. I'm sorry I didn't just say something to you. I am. Please accept that, OK? *(Beat.)* I'm so used to lying to people — you were absolutely right about that — I'm so good at deceiving folks that I just go there most times now. Right off the bat.
BOBBY. That makes sense ... I guess ...
BETTY. Whether it's my colleagues or the kids or Bruce calling me up — I'm always so ready to filter the truth through some other ... whatever. Doesn't matter. This is where I'm at in life. *(Beat.)* ... I need to sit down. *(Betty goes to a couch and sits. Bobby follows after her.)*

BOBBY. You want some water?

BETTY. No, that's OK.

BOBBY. Sure?

BETTY. Yep. I just need to …

BOBBY. I got some pot if you want. Do you?

BETTY. Hmmm?

BOBBY. You know, pot. Weed. Out in the truck if that'd help …

BETTY. Huh. *(Smiles.)* Probably wouldn't hurt any.

BOBBY. I'll grab it. *(He's up and toward the door in two steps. He doubles back and grabs up a box of books. Reaches for his coat — holds it over his head.)* Might as well do a run at the same time.

BETTY. Sure.

BOBBY. Save a little time. Don't worry, I got tarps and shit. *(Beat.)* Right back, Sis.

BETTY. 'Kay. *(Bobby shoots out the open door. Betty sits for a moment, taking in the empty room. Her hand goes to her face, up to her eyes. She covers them. After a moment, she reaches over and snaps on the radio again. A sappy '80s number fills the room. She looks up and quickly turns it off. Bobby returns with a joint — lights it up and takes a good toke. He sits back down, passes it to his sister.)*

BOBBY. Huh?

BETTY. … 's good.

BOBBY. A kid on my block sells it to me cheap. I buy in bulk …

BETTY. Hmmm. So this must not be one of those … you know.

BOBBY. No, what?

BETTY. On your precious list of commandments. "Thou shalt not toke."

BOBBY. Nope. Not that I've ever seen. I try not to read 'em too carefully … *(Smiles at her as he hands over the joint.)* So — and if you don't wanna talk about it, then don't, but …

BETTY. No, go ahead. It's probably better …

BOBBY. Maybe, yeah. *(Beat.)* So, what happened?

BETTY. They don't know.

BOBBY. Really?

BETTY. Uh-uh.

BOBBY. Huh.

BETTY. Not for sure … he was found over on the other side of the lake, there's a bend in the path out where the trees overhang the road and, you know … it gets pretty dark, even during the day. He'd been riding — he loved to ride, that's how he got around, to campus and just as, you know, also as exercise ... so he must've been out doing that. Cycling.

BOBBY. OK. And?

BETTY. And ... we don't know. I spoke to the EMT drivers who brought him in and the police and ... all from the position of a teacher and advisor, of course, but ... and that's all they could say. He was found near his bike, down a sort of grassy slope off the road. He'd hit his head on something and his bike was bent, the back tire, but no obvious cause or time of death.

BOBBY. So, he fell, right? I mean ... that's ...

BETTY. Probably. There weren't any tire marks or some pothole that he no doubt ran into, but he was alone out there, dead ... in the forest ... and it isn't completely clear ...

BOBBY. Huh.

BETTY. Yes.

BOBBY. An animal darted out? Is that possible?

BETTY. It is. It's very curvy out there — you've driven that part of the road, you know — it's dangerous.

BOBBY. Yeah. It can be, sure. Fuck.

BETTY. Anyway, he's ... that's what happened. I'm not really able to push for more because it would just ... it might seem odd.

BOBBY. Sure.

BETTY. So.

BOBBY. And family? You said he's ...

BETTY. They're coming soon. Tomorrow morning.

BOBBY. Really?

BETTY. Yes. *(Beat.)* He's lying there, all alone in the basement of the hospital and I'm afraid to go see him because it wouldn't make any sense to outsiders and there might be ... you know, questions about it, so I don't. I've left him there all alone and, and I'm ashamed that I'm doing that but I'm also scared of what happens if I go. *(Beat.)* See? You always think I'm so in-charge and brave ... but now you can see what a coward I really am.

BOBBY. Don't say that. No, it's not your ...

BETTY. I know. I'm just saying. *(Beat.)* Anyway, I got a call at dinner saying they'd be in tomorrow, so I scrambled to get all this done, but ... and that's when I called you.

BOBBY. This is ... fuck, that's shitty. It really is. I'm sorry for you. *(Beat.)* Honestly.

BETTY. Thanks. Thank you for ... just being ... *(Betty reaches over and gives Bobby a little shoulder rub. It's only a moment and they both smile after. A weird silence between them now. Their faces are close together as they sit there. Bobby reaches over to give his sister a hug. She allows it. They slowly separate. Their lips brush, almost kissing, but they stop. Wait. They go to do it again but this time Betty pushes away. She starts to get up but Bobby pulls her down.)*

BOBBY. No, wait … I'm not … just … WAIT!

BETTY. Don't … Bobby … DON'T! NO!! STOP!!! *(They struggle for another moment and then she breaks off from him. They stand there looking at each other.)* What the hell? Huh? I mean …

BOBBY. Sorry … I wasn't trying to …

BETTY. You hear "stop," you better do it.

BOBBY. That's not what I was …

BETTY. I mean Jesus Christ, I'm your sister …

BOBBY. … I know, Jesus …

BETTY. I don't care if we're smoking pot or not.

BOBBY. That wasn't the … no …

BETTY. You don't have to touch me, Bobby. God!

BOBBY. Fine! Whatever …

BETTY. So fucking … weird … I mean … shit! *(Bobby has had his fill of this conversation. He kicks the coffee table over, spilling magazines everywhere. Gets in his sister's face.)*

BOBBY. … Hey, hey! Just watch your big fucking mouth, OK? Can you do that for me? *(Beat.)* You should be so goddamn lucky and I mean that. You should have God come down from on high and grant you a fucking wish and it should be me. Me or some guy who looks almost exactly like me — same type of dude if you were at all blessed, you hear me? Huh? I mean, you walk around, so pleased with yourself and sure that you're some kind of I-don't-know-what. This lady who everybody wants a piece of but you know what? The only reason anyone feels like that is because they're pretty fucking sure they can … have you, I mean. What the fuck, the rest of the county has, so why not them? You act like some fucking graduate degree erases all your history, you're fooling yourself. *(Beat.)* I've spent most of my life, ever since the first time I walked in on you up in your bedroom there sucking the cock of that kid from our Sunday school — you remember that? Hmmmm? — I've had to watch you make one shit choice after another, the worst mother-fuckers you could find usually, and the nastier they were the better. If Dad didn't like 'em, then that was it far as you were concerned; all the approval you needed. And the little business suits you wear now can't hide the fact that you've got shit for confidence and that you need every guy to like you — was Dad so bad to you, so withholding that you had to end up like some cheap fucking whore who's out on the sidewalk every night, looking for a twenty-dollar blow job? Guess so. *(Beat.)* I don't give a shit what society says about the two of us, brothers and sisters and keep away from each other ... you oughta be happy to have me. Least I'd treat you like a man's supposed to ... not just hoping to fuck you in the ass because you're too drunk to care. Ya know how many times I had to hear that crap in high school? That my sister was fondly remembered not just as the girl who'd put out but the only one that guys could count on to take it in the shitter. 'S nice. Really nice ... *(Beat.)* So don't act like I'm fucking ... crazy because I might've cared about you all these years, wish I could've taken you away from that kinda thing — I'm sorry that I love my sister and, and that I'd do anything for her. Act like I'm sick or some shit because I have feelings — seems like I'm in a lot better place than your husband or, or, any of these other guys, ya know? Sounds like it to me. Just another group a people who wanna use you but not me. I never wanted anything for you but a bunch of good things. Nice, pretty things and you being taken care of. I'm the guy who wanted that for you. I am the person who just wanted you to be a little bit nice and show some kindness to me once in a while ... to act like you needed somebody. This somebody who's your own flesh and blood. *(Beat.)* And you look down your nose at me. That's all you can do, I so much as give you a hug for too long ... push me off like I'm some pervert over at the 7-11 who's got too close to you up by the register. Well, fuck you, that's what I say to that, Betty. Fuck you ... and your very selective morality. You should be grateful to love me and for me to love you. You really should ... *(Beat.)* 'Cause ya certainly don't deserve it — that much I know. No fucking way. *(He stops now and tries to catch his breath. Looks at her. Flash of thunder and lightning. The lights go out. Betty is the first to stand. A glance at her watch again as she crosses to the fuse box. Flick of a switch and lights up.)*

BETTY. ... God, how did it get so late?

BOBBY. So let's take whatever else you need and then you can get back. That's fine.

BETTY. OK, thanks, yes ... ummm, the books and ... I've set a few things on the bed that I can grab and then ... well, also that file cabinet. *(Points.)* Up there.

BOBBY. Alright.

BETTY. That should do it. *(She exits into another room. Returns with a small stack.)*

BOBBY. Great. *(Beat.)* And you don't think…?

BETTY. What?

BOBBY. Nothing. I mean, the family is gonna be here, you don't think they might want … this isn't against you, I'm just saying it … you don't feel like they might be interested in a few of his things?

BETTY. Of course they would be. I hope so.

BOBBY. But not any of his books?

BETTY. No, I think … a lot of these are mine he borrowed or, we … you know, bought when we were together …

BOBBY. I see.

BETTY. So they're … I'd rather just …

BOBBY. You don't wanna leave any evidence.

BETTY. Bobby, please.

BOBBY. I'm not saying anything. I get it … but look at what happened with me. Right? I mean … what if that happened to his mom or dad as they're standing there? With a picture or whatever. What then?

BETTY. I'd … yes. That would be awkward.

BOBBY. So that's why. Really. Isn't it? So just say it, then …

BETTY. What? *(He points over at the stack of loose items she's holding.)*

BOBBY. I know you're doing most of this because of your feelings for the kid but let's be honest — you're covering your own ass. It is only a matter of … whatever until the owner of this place gets nosy and comes down here or, or the police … right? Am I right about that or not, Betty?

BETTY. … Fine. Yes. That, too.

BOBBY. Alright. Just so you know it. *(Beat.)* You oughta try and be a bit more honest with yourself sometimes — 's good for the soul.

BETTY. Because it's important for me to do that now, right? Even after all I've told you?

BOBBY. Just keeping it real, Sis …

BETTY. OK. Are you done?

BOBBY. Yep. Mostly. *(Bobby looks over and points to a stack of valuables as he speaks.)* Lemme ask you this, though: Why are you taking that?

BETTY. ... What?

BOBBY. His laptop. *(Pointing.)* I mean, isn't that kinda risky? I get all the rest of it but something like that — how do you know his parents won't miss that? Wonder where it is and then you'll have to lie about it.

BETTY. No, because ... that's not ...

BOBBY. What? You will ... you'll make up some damn story and then you'll be caught in a ...

BETTY. ... I bought it for him. Last year. It was his birthday and I bought it for him. So.

BOBBY. I see. Still ... I don't see why ...

BETTY. I bought it for him and so I wanna, you know ... keep it as something to remember him by. Is that so hard to understand?

BOBBY. No, it's pretty ... that's quite clear. *(Beat.)* Except you're lying and I don't know why ... *(With a sigh Betty carefully puts down her stack and turns to her brother. Throws her hands up, exasperated.)*

BETTY. God, Bobby ... what do you mean now?! We need to get out of here — can we maybe talk about this after we've...?

BOBBY. Just answer that and I'll hoist all of this other shit up on my shoulders and be gone. 'Kay? No pointing fingers, nothing.

BETTY. Fine. *(Beat.)* What?

BOBBY. That thing's, like, five years old. Maybe more. I have the same one and I know what the new ones look like ...

BETTY. Well, good for you. *(Beat.)* I really don't know what you're driving at. What?

BOBBY. That's a G4 right there. The new ones are something different. Macbook Pros or some shit. They all have a different design ... Up close you can tell but you gotta know what to be looking for. Even I know that.

BETTY. SO WHAT?

BOBBY. Why lie to me about it? That's all I'm saying — just like that ... right here at the end? I don't get it. Can't explain it ...

BETTY. I'm not lying. *(Beat.)* Bobby, look at me — I am telling you the truth. I LEANT HIM THE MONEY TO BUY IT. OK?

BOBBY. I don't care — nobody bought that computer last year. Betty.

BETTY. How do you know that?! Hmm?!! *(Beat.)* You are so damn ... I mean, you're gonna say that to me now, after I open up to you?! Unbelievable! *(Betty goes to pick up the stack again but stops when:)*

47

BOBBY. What, you got your boyfriend some used computer? Is that the story?

BETTY. It is possible, isn't it? They do still sell them … I mean, people out there, on Craig's List or, or eBay or whatever … IT COULD BE TRUE, RIGHT?

BOBBY. Maybe. I'd be surprised, though … somebody who rents this guy a place and buys him all these books …

BETTY. I didn't say that I personally got on … fuck, Columbo! WHAT IS YOUR POINT?!

BOBBY. I'm just saying! You paint a certain deal when you're talking about him, all these glowing memories and then … I dunno. This one just doesn't fit. And I question it. *(Betty stands and looks at her brother. Who is this guy?)*

BETTY. What're you saying to me? I think that … you want to say something so just do. GO AHEAD.

BOBBY. OK. I will. Because I'm nothing if not a fucking honest guy. Mostly. Try to be.

BETTY. Just … OK, what? Seriously, WHAT?

BOBBY. I think you're still holding shit back from me. Obviously from everybody else but even from this conversation we had here. Tonight.

BETTY. Yeah?

BOBBY. I do. I feel it and I believe it's true.

BETTY. Well, you think what you want. I need to get home …

BOBBY. I think there's something on that laptop you don't want people to know about.

BETTY. …

BOBBY. Am I right?

BETTY. This is … why do you have to do this to me? Right now? Huh?!

BOBBY. I'm not doing anything that you didn't do already. This is your mess, Sis. This one right here … it's all yours. Like usual. You fuck shit up and then you want it to be all better, to just go away … well, it doesn't, Betty. OK? Bad-shit-lives-on and you can't outrun it. You can't.

BETTY. I just … I bought him this computer! Gave him the money to purchase it, and he …

BOBBY. No, you didn't. That just isn't true …

BETTY. You don't know everything!!

BOBBY. I know enough. I know that machine is not new and …

well, doesn't matter. *(Beat.)* So why?

BETTY. … because.

BOBBY. Yeah, I know there's a reason. I'd like to hear it, now that I know I'm looting the house of a dead man. Destroying evidence.

BETTY. Please don't talk like that.

BOBBY. Then tell me. NOW.

BETTY. AAAHHHH!!! You're right … OK?! Feel better? You are right about this …

BOBBY. About what?

BETTY. It's his. I wanted to buy him a new one, was going to but he had all his … shit … on this one, you know how people can be about their own — he was always so particular about his computer and all his whatever, I dunno, his, his iPhone and …

BOBBY. Yeah. And?

BETTY. And he didn't want it … I got him a gift certificate instead. I did that but I was going to buy him the one you mentioned … the Mac-something. Pro.

BOBBY. OK. Fine. So why are you…?

BETTY. Because, Bobby! Shit. Isn't it obvious?

BOBBY. It's getting to be … yeah. GO ON.

BETTY. There ended up being things … some stuff on it that wasn't … doesn't matter! Just things. Thing all over this place that I want to get rid of. *(Beat.)* And that's not all … I mean, God knows what's up in that file cabinet that he kept locked for some reason … so … just …

BOBBY. I think it does.

BETTY. What?

BOBBY. I bet it does matter. All this stuff.

BETTY. Oh, for God's sake! STOP! Just …

BOBBY. No, I'm not going to …

BETTY. Bobby!

BOBBY. We're gonna do this right now and I don't give a shit what you think. You put me in the middle of this so here we go. You're gonna tell me EVERYTHING YOU KNOW. NOW. *(Betty shakes her head — drifting a bit before she speaks.)*

BETTY. There are files on there I wouldn't want his parents — or anybody else, really seeing. Emails from me and just other things. OK? *(Beat.)* A couple pictures … I also found out that — by peeking at a time that I shouldn't've, when he wasn't aware of it — I saw … things of his that were … other girls on there … Facebook and that sort of deal … he was friendly with many more people than I was led to believe. So that was another thing … my golden boy wasn't as lovely and shiny as I'd imagined him to be. *(Beat.)* And then there was one more find, too …

BOBBY. What's that?

BETTY. It was so simple … just a few little bits of his diary … notes that he kept with all his thoughts and wishes and dreams …

BOBBY. Yeah? And?

BETTY. … And I wasn't one of them. I was — how did he put it? — "Old" and "expendable." "OK in bed," he wrote. "Sex with her is like fucking gray Jell-O." *(Beat.)* Ha! For so long I have been chased and wanted and a prize … and now some boy … this second-year senior reduces me to nothing in just a few words. Less than nothing. Jell-O. Well, you can imagine how something like that might take your breath away …

BOBBY. … I'm sure.

BETTY. I suddenly saw what it was like to become invisible. You know? To be seen through. *(Beat.)* I mean, I felt it coming — "campus" is not for the weak of heart, trust me … new, beautiful girls every term, year in and out, and yet … I could still turn a head or two. You know, when I tried. Some makeup on and my heels or whatever, yeah. I still had a little something. But hey, college guys are easy, I suppose — looking to get laid and they don't really care by who, so that wasn't any great accomplishment. Still, didn't hurt at eight A.M. as you're walking across the lawn there. A bunch of guys whistle at you … it's stupid, but it at least makes you feel alive or whatnot. Wanted. Even just for a second. *(Beat.)* So with him … this beautiful young guy who I find in my office one day, needs help on a scholarship application and he makes me smile and laugh and, and he's … he likes my "hair" … it doesn't take long. To get sucked in. To believe in something, even if you know it's probably not the truth. You want it so bad, need to believe in that illusion so, so much because it's all you ever were — this pretty face and a girl who would say "yes" — it's not so easy to give that up. For it to pass you by. And so later, you'll do almost anything to keep it, to hear it again just once. And from whomever. Kid down at the pharmacy. Some old man getting his coffee in Dunkin' Donuts. That's how pathetic ya get. Shit. *(Beat.)* But it does pass. Yes, it does and one day you are transparent. People walk by and don't see you, they say, "Excuse me, ma'am," and you just want to scream, you wanna grab them and shake them and yell, "I am a fucking beautiful, desirable woman," but you don't. You don't do anything like it because you've started to know, inside somewhere you've begun to recognize the truth. You are not that anymore. You're just normal now and, and middle-aged and tired most of the day and everyone, from your husband on down, has begun to see right past you. Through you. As if you're no longer even there. *(Beat.)* I'm not making any excuses here, Bobby, but I'm just saying. I'm saying that's how it is for me these days, that's all ... *(Betty looks at him but past him, too. Lost in thought. Silence for a moment.)* And that's everything, Bobby. I promise.

BOBBY. Yeah?

BETTY. Yes. That is the truth — as ugly and as, you now ... terrible as it seems. That is what has happened. And why I'm doing all this.

BOBBY. I see.

BETTY. So now you know. *(Beat.)* I don't care what you say ... I gave myself to this boy. I believed in him. In us. *(Beat.)* I hadn't done that in a long time. Trusted someone like that ... and he ... he said he was staying another year for me ... so that we would ... taking time to finish his thesis for me. So he could be with me, he said.

BOBBY. I'm sure. *(Bobby doesn't know what else to say but knows enough to keep his big mouth shut at the right moments.)*

BETTY. He did! That we might — it seemed like he was offering me this whole new universe but — instead he shit on that ... *(Beat.)* I know I did a lot of bad things to get here and so why should it work out for me, but I just ... *(Beat.)* I did love him, Bobby. That is not a lie ... I loved him and he was using me. I wasn't ever going to be anything but a footnote to him. In the end. *(Beat.)* And then, just to make the entire thing pointless and painful and sad ... this past weekend, on a beautiful afternoon ... he was out biking and he died. *(Bobby turns to Betty and looks at her. Long and hard. He nods, thinking carefully before speaking.)*

BOBBY. He was out biking ...

BETTY. ... Yes ... around the lake ...

BOBBY. And he died.

BETTY. He did. Yes.

BOBBY. Oh. *(Betty shakes her head dimly. Lost in all of her thoughts.)*

BETTY. They're continuing to investigate ... said they'll be in touch, but ... for now ...

BOBBY. I see.

BETTY. So you never know. I can't ask about it without people being suspicious ...

BOBBY. Yeah, you said that.

BETTY. And his parents are coming — I told you all that, didn't I? Did I?

BOBBY. Yes ... "tomorrow," you said.

BETTY. That's right. I spoke to the father.

BOBBY. Uh-huh.

BETTY. And I wanted to give away a lot of this stuff — books and things — but we already talked about that.

BOBBY. Yes.

BETTY. So you know what I'm doing? Right?

BOBBY. You want to get your things outta here before they show up. Before anyone can come over here and start — I get it. It's understandable.

BETTY. Is it?

BOBBY. Sure. What good does it do for everybody if your relationship came out now? Right? It's just sadness, that's all this'd be, especially for his family. And yours.

BETTY. Exactly! That's what I thought, so I ... that's why I tried to get all the ...

BOBBY. You did this.

BETTY. Yes. Came here after calling you up. I am trying to do a good thing ...

BOBBY. I get it now. I do ... *(Beat.)* So just one more question.

BETTY. OK. I'm getting tired, though ...

BOBBY. Just hold on. Just this. Tell me now — tell me one true thing and I will help you in any way I can. I promise ... *(Beat.)* He died in the afternoon, you just said.

BETTY. Yes.

BOBBY. But before ... before you said they didn't know how. Or when. That it was ...

BETTY. No. I don't think they do. Nope. *(He looks long and hard at Betty. The truth is just ahead.)*

BOBBY. I see ... *(Beat.)* Then how did you know it was in the afternoon? Betty? I mean, how could you possibly know that? Hmmm? *(She stares up at him silently. Only her eyes blinking rapidly.)*

BETTY. ... I dunno.

BOBBY. And I'm not saying anything here, I'm not some cop, but ... if he did hit a bump or, like, some shitty patch of pavement out there OR an animal, some fucking squirrel, a deer, whatever, jumped out in front of him — and maybe it did, it's possible —

BETTY. ... They think that's what happened ...

BOBBY. Yeah, I heard that before, I did, but ... if that was the case? How come it's his back tire that's messed up now and not the front one? Why would that be? *(Beat.)* I want you to think about that ... *(Betty doesn't say anything — just keeps looking at Bobby.)* You didn't scratch your car at the store, did you?

BETTY. ...

BOBBY. Did you?

BETTY. What?

BOBBY. Betty?

BETTY. I don't know ... I don't remember now.

BOBBY. Yes, you do. YOU DO KNOW.

BETTY. I do?

BOBBY. Say it to me and I'll help you. Just come clean for one time — and I mean, with all of your stuff, the whole pile of fucking shit you carry around — do that and I can help you ...

BETTY. I'm ... I'm not sure that ... I ...

BOBBY. Say it.

BETTY. ... But ...

BOBBY. Come on!

BETTY. I can't ... Bobby ... I can't do that ... *(He grabs her by the shoulders and shakes her. Violently.)*

BOBBY. Yes, you can! Say it, Betty. SAY IT TO ME NOW, GOD-DAMNIT! JUST SAY IT!!

BETTY. Owww! You're hurting me!! STOP!!

BOBBY. Then say the fucking words!

BETTY. ... No ...

BOBBY. SAY-IT! SAY THE TRUTH OR I SWEAR TO GOD THAT I'LL...!!

BETTY. Stop it! Stop yelling at me!!

BOBBY. Then do it! Come on, just do it!!

BETTY. I can't!

BOBBY. Yes, you can, people can do anything they want, they do it all the time and so can you! YES!!

BETTY. No, Bobby, stop it ... stop!

BOBBY. No! I'm not stopping this time, I'm not!

BETTY. Leave me alone!

BOBBY. Tell me the truth! Say what you've done!

BETTY. No! Stop it, no!! I'm not gonna — *(Bobby lets go of Betty and goes to the door and swings it open. The rain pouring down.)*
BOBBY. I WILL WALK OUT RIGHT NOW, WALK THE FUCK OUT AND LEAVE YOU HERE!! YOU WANT THAT?! HUH?!! DO-YOU-WANT-THAT?!!!
BETTY. ... I'm ...
BOBBY. DO YOU?! IS THAT WHAT YOU WANT, BETTY?!!
BETTY. ... I don't know anymore!
BOBBY. ... Then fine. That's ... you know what? You're on your own. Just how you like it. *(Nothing from Betty. Bobby slowly turns and starts to go out. At the last moment, Betty calls out to him:.)*
BETTY. Please don't! Bobby! PLEASE!!
BOBBY. *(Turning.)* ... What?
BETTY. Please. I'm not ... *(Starts to cry.)* I need you. OK? I'm asking now because ... I just really do need you. PLEASE. DON'T LEAVE ME HERE. I CAN'T ... I'M ... PLEASE DON'T ... *(Bobby closes the door and turns back to his sister. After a long silence:)*
BOBBY. So tell me then. Say it now. The truth. *(A long silence. Betty finally speaks up and breaks it.)*
BETTY. I was never at the store. Or by ... what'd you call it? The thingie there.
BOBBY. Cart corral?
BETTY. Yes. That. *(Tries to smile.)* ... Bobby, I can't ... it's so hard to be ... I didn't go to the store that day. That's all I can say ... is I didn't ... *(Bobby lets this soak in — he looks around the room, taking it all in. This time in the harsh light of reality. For a second it looks like the truth is too much to take — Bobby braces himself and lets the emotion pass, but Betty bursts into tears. After a moment:)*
BOBBY. So listen to me — I'm gonna pack up the rest of this shit and I'm gonna take it back to my place. Leave it in the garage.
BETTY. OK.
BOBBY. Did you hear me?
BETTY. Yes. I think so.
BOBBY. Betty, fucking listen right now! OK?
BETTY. ... I am. You're taking it all with you. *(Beat.)* Thank you.
BOBBY. Yeah, and I'm ... tomorrow morning I want to see your car. OK? I want you to bring it over to my place and I'm gonna take care of those marks on it ...
BETTY. We can ... but Bruce said we can always ...
BOBBY. Fuck Bruce. He's not here now — you didn't go to Bruce

with this. You listen to me and do what I say, all right? Take it to my house tomorrow and I'll fix it for you …

BETTY. You will?

BOBBY. I can sand that down and repaint it and I think it'll be fine. You hear me? Soon as you can, OK?

BETTY. Alright.

BOBBY. Yes? First thing.

BETTY. … I will.

BOBBY. You should go home now. Right now. I can do the rest and I'll take the keys …

BETTY. Really?

BOBBY. Yeah. I got it. Just go.

BETTY. I will, in a second. I just need to rest for a minute.

BOBBY. OK. But hurry. You need to go.

BETTY. But … if you do…?

BOBBY. What? I can lock a fucking door. Promise.

BETTY. No … the other. If you do that — help me — is it a sin, Bobby? Is it? *(Bobby stops and looks at her. A funny look on his face as he finally shrugs his shoulders.)*

BOBBY. You know what? I dunno anymore.

BETTY. You don't?

BOBBY. Nope. I do not know that answer.

BETTY. Well, that's a first …

BOBBY. Yeah, it's true. I know a lot of shit, but not that one.

BETTY. It's not a commandment or anything, is it?

BOBBY. Betty … I'm not even gonna check. I don't know and I'm not gonna look into it right now … so …

BETTY. OK.

BOBBY. It is what it is. It's me helping out my sister, that's all I can see.

BETTY. Thank you. Because I do need you … I do.

BOBBY. I know you do.

BETTY. Thank you … Bobby. Thank you.

BOBBY. … You're welcome, Sis. *(Bobby walks over to where Betty is sitting. Stands above her. He reaches down and touches her hair. He brushes it slightly. Betty smiles. Looks up at her brother for a moment, then leans her head against his hand. One real moment finally passes between them. Bobby goes to the stairs and climbs quickly up into the loft. Grabs the file cabinet and hoists it up into the air and tosses it over the railing to the floor. Smash! The sound is deafening and Betty jumps.*

Looks up. Bobby comes downstairs, grabs it up and starts out the door. Scoops up the laptop on his way out.)

BETTY. ... Bobby? Do you ... you wanna at least know his name or anything like that?

BOBBY. No. I don't. I don't wanna know anything about 'im. Alright? Just ... *(She nods. A crack of thunder. The lights flicker and go out. The rest happens by candlelight.).* It's OK, don't worry. I can still see what I'm doing ...

BETTY. 'Kay. *(Beat.)* Hey, Bobby...?

BOBBY. What?

BETTY. The truth ...

BOBBY. Uh-huh? What about it?

BETTY. It hurts ... don't it?

BOBBY. Yeah, it does. It stings like a bitch. *(Smiles.)* That's why they call it that ... *(They look at each other for a moment. She nods. He exits. Betty sits on the couch. Turns to the radio and turns it on. Something like Modern English singing "Melt with You."* She smiles lightly and closes her eyes. Puts her head back onto the cushion. Betty resting. Lights slowly fading. Music blaring. Silence. Darkness.)*

End of Play

---

* See Special Note on Songs and Recordings on copyright page.

PROPERTY LIST

Boxes, books, magazines
Candles, matches
Six-pack of Bud
Towel
Money
Wine glass
Framed photo
Book with photo
Cell phone
Purse with cell phone
Joint
Laptop
File cabinet

SOUND EFFECTS

Rain
'80s music
Thunder
Cell phone rings

NEW PLAYS

★ **MOTHERHOOD OUT LOUD by Leslie Ayvazian, Brooke Berman, David Cale, Jessica Goldberg, Beth Henley, Lameece Issaq, Claire LaZebnik, Lisa Loomer, Michele Lowe, Marco Pennette, Theresa Rebeck, Luanne Rice, Annie Weisman and Cheryl L. West, conceived by Susan R. Rose and Joan Stein.** When entrusting the subject of motherhood to such a dazzling collection of celebrated American writers, what results is a joyous, moving, hilarious, and altogether thrilling theatrical event. "Never fails to strike both the funny bone and the heart." *–BackStage.* "Packed with wisdom, laughter, and plenty of wry surprises." *–TheaterMania.* [1M, 3W] ISBN: 978-0-8222-2589-8

★ **COCK by Mike Bartlett.** When John takes a break from his boyfriend, he accidentally meets the girl of his dreams. Filled with guilt and indecision, he decides there is only one way to straighten this out. "[A] brilliant and blackly hilarious feat of provocation." *–Independent.* "A smart, prickly and rewarding view of sexual and emotional confusion." *–Evening Standard.* [3M, 1W] ISBN: 978-0-8222-2766-3

★ **F. Scott Fitzgerald's THE GREAT GATSBY adapted for the stage by Simon Levy.** Jay Gatsby, a self-made millionaire, passionately pursues the elusive Daisy Buchanan. Nick Carraway, a young newcomer to Long Island, is drawn into their world of obsession, greed and danger. "Levy's combination of narration, dialogue and action delivers most of what is best in the novel." *–Seattle Post-Intelligencer.* "A beautifully crafted interpretation of the 1925 novel which defined the Jazz Age." *–London Free Press.* [5M, 4W] ISBN: 978-0-8222-2727-4

★ **LONELY, I'M NOT by Paul Weitz.** At an age when most people are discovering what they want to do with their lives, Porter has been married and divorced, earned seven figures as a corporate "ninja," and had a nervous breakdown. It's been four years since he's had a job or a date, and he's decided to give life another shot. "Critic's pick!" *–NY Times.* "An enjoyable ride." *–NY Daily News.* [3M, 3W] ISBN: 978-0-8222-2734-2

★ **ASUNCION by Jesse Eisenberg.** Edgar and Vinny are not racist. In fact, Edgar maintains a blog condemning American imperialism, and Vinny is three-quarters into a Ph.D. in Black Studies. When Asuncion becomes their new roommate, the boys have a perfect opportunity to demonstrate how open-minded they truly are. "Mr. Eisenberg writes lively dialogue that strikes plenty of comic sparks." *–NY Times.* "An almost ridiculously enjoyable portrait of slacker trauma among would-be intellectuals." *–Newsday.* [2M, 2W] ISBN: 978-0-8222-2630-7

DRAMATISTS PLAY SERVICE, INC.
440 Park Avenue South, New York, NY 10016 212-683-8960 Fax 212-213-1539
postmaster@dramatists.com   www.dramatists.com

NEW PLAYS

★ **THE PICTURE OF DORIAN GRAY by Roberto Aguirre-Sacasa, based on the novel by Oscar Wilde.** Preternaturally handsome Dorian Gray has his portrait painted by his college classmate Basil Hallwood. When their mutual friend Henry Wotton offers to include it in a show, Dorian makes a fateful wish—that his portrait should grow old instead of him—and strikes an unspeakable bargain with the devil. [5M, 2W] ISBN: 978-0-8222-2590-4

★ **THE LYONS by Nicky Silver.** As Ben Lyons lies dying, it becomes clear that he and his wife have been at war for many years, and his impending demise has brought no relief. When they're joined by their children all efforts at a sentimental goodbye to the dying patriarch are soon abandoned. "Hilariously frank, clear-sighted, compassionate and forgiving." *–NY Times.* "Mordant, dark and rich." *–Associated Press.* [3M, 3W] ISBN: 978-0-8222-2659-8

★ **STANDING ON CEREMONY by Mo Gaffney, Jordan Harrison, Moisés Kaufman, Neil LaBute, Wendy MacLeod, José Rivera, Paul Rudnick, and Doug Wright, conceived by Brian Shnipper.** Witty, warm and occasionally wacky, these plays are vows to the blessings of equality, the universal challenges of relationships and the often hilarious power of love. "CEREMONY puts a human face on a hot-button issue and delivers laughter and tears rather than propaganda." *–BackStage.* [3M, 3W] ISBN: 978-0-8222-2654-3

★ **ONE ARM by Moisés Kaufman, based on the short story and screenplay by Tennessee Williams.** Ollie joins the Navy and becomes the lightweight boxing champion of the Pacific Fleet. Soon after, he loses his arm in a car accident, and he turns to hustling to survive. "[A] fast, fierce, brutally beautiful stage adaptation." *–NY Magazine.* "A fascinatingly lurid, provocative and fatalistic piece of theater." *–Variety.* [7M, 1W] ISBN: 978-0-8222-2564-5

★ **AN ILIAD by Lisa Peterson and Denis O'Hare.** A modern-day retelling of Homer's classic. Poetry and humor, the ancient tale of the Trojan War and the modern world collide in this captivating theatrical experience. "Shocking, glorious, primal and deeply satisfying." *–Time Out NY.* "Explosive, altogether breathtaking." *–Chicago Sun-Times.* [1M] ISBN: 978-0-8222-2687-1

★ **THE COLUMNIST by David Auburn.** At the height of the Cold War, Joe Alsop is the nation's most influential journalist, beloved, feared and courted by the Washington world. But as the '60s dawn and America undergoes dizzying change, the intense political dramas Joe is embroiled in become deeply personal as well. "Intensely satisfying." *–Bloomberg News.* [5M, 2W] ISBN: 978-0-8222-2699-4

DRAMATISTS PLAY SERVICE, INC.
440 Park Avenue South, New York, NY 10016 212-683-8960 Fax 212-213-1539
postmaster@dramatists.com   www.dramatists.com

NEW PLAYS

★ **BENGAL TIGER AT THE BAGHDAD ZOO by Rajiv Joseph.** The lives of two American Marines and an Iraqi translator are forever changed by an encounter with a quick-witted tiger who haunts the streets of war-torn Baghdad. "[A] boldly imagined, harrowing and surprisingly funny drama." *–NY Times.* "Tragic yet darkly comic and highly imaginative." *–CurtainUp.* [5M, 2W] ISBN: 978-0-8222-2565-2

★ **THE PITMEN PAINTERS by Lee Hall, inspired by a book by William Feaver.** Based on the triumphant true story, a group of British miners discover a new way to express themselves and unexpectedly become art-world sensations. "Excitingly ambiguous, in-the-moment theater." *–NY Times.* "Heartfelt, moving and deeply politicized." *–Chicago Tribune.* [5M, 2W] ISBN: 978-0-8222-2507-2

★ **RELATIVELY SPEAKING by Ethan Coen, Elaine May and Woody Allen.** In TALKING CURE, Ethan Coen uncovers the sort of insanity that can only come from family. Elaine May explores the hilarity of passing in GEORGE IS DEAD. In HONEYMOON MOTEL, Woody Allen invites you to the sort of wedding day you won't forget. "Firecracker funny." *–NY Times.* "A rollicking good time." *–New Yorker.* [8M, 7W] ISBN: 978-0-8222-2394-8

★ **SONS OF THE PROPHET by Stephen Karam.** If to live is to suffer, then Joseph Douaihy is more alive than most. With unexplained chronic pain and the fate of his reeling family on his shoulders, Joseph's health, sanity, and insurance premium are on the line. "Explosively funny." *–NY Times.* "At once deep, deft and beautifully made." *–New Yorker.* [5M, 3W] ISBN: 978-0-8222-2597-3

★ **THE MOUNTAINTOP by Katori Hall.** A gripping reimagination of events the night before the assassination of the civil rights leader Dr. Martin Luther King, Jr. "An ominous electricity crackles through the opening moments." *–NY Times.* "[A] thrilling, wild, provocative flight of magical realism." *–Associated Press.* "Crackles with theatricality and a humanity more moving than sainthood." *–NY Newsday.* [1M, 1W] ISBN: 978-0-8222-2603-1

★ **ALL NEW PEOPLE by Zach Braff.** Charlie is 35, heartbroken, and just wants some time away from the rest of the world. Long Beach Island seems to be the perfect escape until his solitude is interrupted by a motley parade of misfits who show up and change his plans. "Consistently and sometimes sensationally funny." *–NY Times.* "A morbidly funny play about the trendy new existential condition of being young, adorable, and miserable." *–Variety.* [2M, 2W] ISBN: 978-0-8222-2562-1

DRAMATISTS PLAY SERVICE, INC.
440 Park Avenue South, New York, NY 10016 212-683-8960 Fax 212-213-1539
postmaster@dramatists.com www.dramatists.com

NEW PLAYS

★ **CLYBOURNE PARK by Bruce Norris.** WINNER OF THE 2011 PULITZER PRIZE AND 2012 TONY AWARD. Act One takes place in 1959 as community leaders try to stop the sale of a home to a black family. Act Two is set in the same house in the present day as the now predominantly African-American neighborhood battles to hold its ground. "Vital, sharp-witted and ferociously smart." –*NY Times.* "A theatrical treasure…Indisputably, uproariously funny." –*Entertainment Weekly.* [4M, 3W] ISBN: 978-0-8222-2697-0

★ **WATER BY THE SPOONFUL by Quiara Alegría Hudes.** WINNER OF THE 2012 PULITZER PRIZE. A Puerto Rican veteran is surrounded by the North Philadelphia demons he tried to escape in the service. "This is a very funny, warm, and yes uplifting play." –*Hartford Courant.* "The play is a combination poem, prayer and app on how to cope in an age of uncertainty, speed and chaos." –*Variety.* [4M, 3W] ISBN: 978-0-8222-2716-8

★ **RED by John Logan.** WINNER OF THE 2010 TONY AWARD. Mark Rothko has just landed the biggest commission in the history of modern art. But when his young assistant, Ken, gains the confidence to challenge him, Rothko faces the agonizing possibility that his crowning achievement could also become his undoing. "Intense and exciting." –*NY Times.* "Smart, eloquent entertainment." –*New Yorker.* [2M] ISBN: 978-0-8222-2483-9

★ **VENUS IN FUR by David Ives.** Thomas, a beleaguered playwright/director, is desperate to find an actress to play Vanda, the female lead in his adaptation of the classic sadomasochistic tale *Venus in Fur*. "Ninety minutes of good, kinky fun." –*NY Times.* "A fast-paced journey into one man's entrapment by a clever, vengeful female." –*Associated Press.* [1M, 1W] ISBN: 978-0-8222-2603-1

★ **OTHER DESERT CITIES by Jon Robin Baitz.** Brooke returns home to Palm Springs after a six-year absence and announces that she is about to publish a memoir dredging up a pivotal and tragic event in the family's history—a wound they don't want reopened. "Leaves you feeling both moved and gratifyingly sated." –*NY Times.* "A genuine pleasure." –*NY Post.* [2M, 3W] ISBN: 978-0-8222-2605-5

★ **TRIBES by Nina Raine.** Billy was born deaf into a hearing family and adapts brilliantly to his family's unconventional ways, but it's not until he meets Sylvia, a young woman on the brink of deafness, that he finally understands what it means to be understood. "A smart, lively play." –*NY Times.* "[A] bright and boldly provocative drama." –*Associated Press.* [3M, 2W] ISBN: 978-0-8222-2751-9

DRAMATISTS PLAY SERVICE, INC.
440 Park Avenue South, New York, NY 10016 212-683-8960 Fax 212-213-1539
postmaster@dramatists.com www.dramatists.com